MEMORIES OF THE FUTURE

Why Are We Here On Earth?

Robert S. Van Santen
Marguerite V. Miller

TO SOW THE FALLOW SOIL

Winston-Derek Publishers, Inc.
Pennywell Drive—P.O. Box 90883
Nashville, TN 37209

First printing

Cover design by Morgan Pickard

PUBLISHED BY WINSTON-DEREK PUBLISHERS, INC.
Nashville, Tennessee 37205

Library of Congress Catalog Card No: 89-52124
ISBN: 1-55523-308-2

Printed in the United States of America

Thanks for your friendship.

With kind regards

Robert Van Sauter

FOR OUR CHILDREN, GRANDCHILDREN, AND THEIR FUTURE.

TABLE OF CONTENTS

I

MEMORIES OF THE FUTURE

A child is born or a friend dies. Suddenly we are confronted with realities of life which ordinarily pass unnoticed. At crucial moments such as these we come face to face with our own mortality. Timeless questions well up in us:

> What is the meaning of life?
> Is there purpose to life?
> Is life significant?
> Is there hope?

Throughout history the most modest men to the wisest philosophers have looked for answers to these same enigmas. Yet, it is clear from the way the questions continue to live in us, the answers they have offered us do not satisfy our need to know. There may come moments when we resign ourselves to the idea the answers to our questions cannot be found. In fact, the reason true and satisfying explanations have not been uncovered is quite simple. The answers have been hidden from us, concealed. However, we do not have to look very far to find them.

We will come to realize that answers to the riddles of life cannot be discovered if we only look within the boundaries of one lifetime. If we have the courage to persevere beyond these boundaries, we will find that the idea of reincarnation emerges. By reincarnation we do not mean humans return to earth as plants or animals, but rather that humans return after death to new and repeated human lives. The idea of reincarnation offers us possibilities for uncovering the answers we seek. In our time this idea of reincarnation is finding its way into mainstream thought. People from many walks of life are openly admitting their belief that we repeatedly return to an earthly existence after death. We too will find the idea of reincarnation to be a fruitful point of departure for our exploration. It is imperative to understand that the most significant point of reincarnation is not our reappearance in a renewed life on earth. The key to unraveling the mysteries of life lies in the logical consequence of repeated earth lives—we exist before birth and after death. The region where we reside during these periods is the spiritual world; it is our true homeland. This means the origin of human life is spiritual. Life on earth is only a fragment of the enigma of existence. We were spiritual entities before we were born and we will resume a spiritual existence after we die. Our homeland is not the material world, but rather the spiritual world. This is the most fundamental reality of human life. However, we gain nothing in our search for answers to these eternal questions by blindly accepting this idea of reincarnation.

If we want to discover the meaning of life, our investigation must begin at the cardinal point that our homeland is the spiritual world. Blind faith can have no place in our search. Only objective thinking and common sense will be expected. While reading, there may come moments when you know with an undeniable certainty you have discovered something absolutely true, something irrefutably correct. The certainty of this recognition may feel like the recollection of a long forgotten memory. For each person this instant will be different. This memory of the future will become a point of reference around which all ideas will come into focus.

Pause once in a while to question what is said, especially those ideas that are unfamiliar to you. Be honest, think through the ideas we put forth, then draw your own conclusions about them. The outcome of your thoughts and reflections could be contrary to some of your existing beliefs and assumptions. If that happens you may need to be brave and accept the consequences of what and where your thinking has brought you. When we realize that our homeland is the region where we exist before birth and after death, our perception of what occurs in life and in the world will change dramatically. With these concepts as our foundation, we may find that life on earth at last can become understandable.

Most of the ideas portrayed in this book are based on the spiritual insights of Rudolf Steiner as expressed in his Anthroposophy; others are the result of our own investigations.

And now, let us start on our path of discovery.

II

Our Origin is Celestial

We began our discussion by presuming that we exist before we are born into a physical body and continue to exist after death. We said that our origin is celestial. Every religious denomination teaches that when we are born we are endowed with eternal substance. Religion also tells us that after death this eternal substance is released from the physical body and once again has an independent spiritual existence. However, for countless people the idea of a spiritual existence no longer strikes a meaningful, responsive chord. For them, the divine reality of this truth has been lost. How then, can we still find this reality and know with any certainty that in addition to an earthly life, we also have a spiritual life?

The evidence we have of our earthly existence is that we are born, we live on earth and one day we die. That is as far as we can go in proving we have an earthly life. Evidence of an existence before birth will be difficult to find if we only look for it in the same materialistic, nuts-and-bolts way. However, if we approach even the most fundamental events of everyday life with sensitivity and consciousness we can find abundant evidence of our spiritual origin.

Let's begin by looking at birth. Birth is the most basic confirmation of the reality of our physical existence. Looked at anew, birth can also provide evidence of our spiritual origin. Ask any mother what impressions she had of her baby before it was born. We will find that most mothers had an accurate sense of the temperament of the child they were carrying. They relate stories of babies who were very active before birth and who became busy, lively infants. Others were placid before birth. After birth this characteristic manifested even more strongly in mild-mannered, dreamy children. It is not unusual to hear such stories. Mothers are almost always aware that the nature and character of their child was evident to them before birth. From baby pictures of children and adults we know, we can see in their newborn features as well, the character which later became prominent. If our character can already manifest itself before birth and in the first moments of our life, it has to be more than the expression of our social surrounding and our genetic make up. Where does it come from? The truth is that we carry our character with us into this earthly life from our spiritual home. Our character is the echoed expression of our experiences during our former lives and our experiences in the spiritual world. If this were not the case, how could we explain that parents who have more than one child find that the character of each is so completely different from the others. If we were the product solely of our inherited background or our circumstances in this life, there would be no reason why each of us would turn out to be such remarkably unique individuals.

Other evidence of an existence beyond earthly life can be found if we investigate our need to sleep. Most everyone agrees that during sleep our ordinary, daily consciousness is suspended. A doctor or scientist can give detailed explanations of the physiology and psychology of sleep. He can relate the most complicated bio-chemical explanations of what happens to our brain and body while we sleep. He will even go so far as to say that a prolonged period without sleep can cause severe mental imbalance. But he cannot explain why we need to sleep or why sleep prevents the imbalance. If we look at the explanations science offers, it is clear that its conclusions are based on the idea that sleep is a result of exhaustion. Entire libraries have been written about sleep based on this idea. Still science offers no explanation of why we tire and why we need to eventually—even spontaneously—fall asleep. If what science has concluded were true, how could we explain that small babies need more sleep than anyone?

The reality of our need to sleep is not so difficult to discover. A simple metaphor can bring us closer to a more fruitful understanding. Think of a fish and its natural habitat. Fish are water-beings; they cannot live out of water. If we were to remove a fish from water, it would survive, but only for a short time. Left out of water indefinitely, it would become faint and die. If we throw it back in time, it will regain its equilibrium and swim away unharmed. Humans have a similar relationship to the spiritual world. Just as the fish cannot live for a substantial time out of its natural surrounding—the water, we cannot live for an extended period of time away from our natural surrounding, the spiritual world. We can be separated from the spiritual world only temporarily. When we are separated for too long an interval we feel tired (or we could say faint, like the fish). This is the reality of our need to sleep. We are fundamentally spiritual beings who must return regularly to our spiritual surrounding. Sleep is the way we maintain our continuing connection with our spiritual origin.

Another analogy will help us to appreciate this reality even more. Think of the human being as a sponge. During sleep we immerse ourselves in the spiritual world and soak up the living, restorative, spiritual substance found there. When we are awake we gradually wring out this substance during our daily activities until there is hardly any spiritual substance left. In this depleted state we feel the need to reconnect with the spiritual world. We fall asleep. During sleep we once again replenish our spiritual substance so that when we awake we are refreshed and full of energy.

This illustrates that in actuality we are merely visitors on the earth who return to our homeland—the spiritual world—during sleep. At first this idea might seem preposterous. However, if we reflect on life with this idea in mind, we can see for ourselves that the events of life reveal more than just a surface reality. The truth of this idea and its inherent logic will become ever more apparent and will help us in our search.

What does it mean that our origin is spiritual? It indicates that the essence of our being does not belong to the earth, that our birthplace and homeland are in the spiritual world. While we live on earth we are composed of a physical body as well as spiritual components. Our fundamental spiritual member, which we call our spirit or ego, is eternal. (NOTE: We use the word spirit for our eternal part when it resides in the spiritual world; during life on earth we use the word ego. In reality there is no difference between ego and spirit). Our ego resides temporarily in a physical body during earthly existence, and continues to exist when this physical body is discarded at death. Our ego progresses from incarnation to incarnation, maturing with every new re-embodiment. Our ego—or spirit—is our authentic, eternal being. During the time between death and rebirth it is our ego that plans the tasks of the next life and makes the decision to return to earth in a bodily form. The reasons we want to return to a new incarnation are complex. We need to investigate them step by step.

The spiritual world is a realm in which there is no falsehood or deception. Cosmic truth reigns in the spiritual world. Without exception everything in this cosmic realm is dictated by cosmic law. Lies, untruths, pretense, concealment do not—indeed, cannot—exist there. Cosmic laws are fixed and cannot be bent or broken, they simply ARE. In the cosmos, where everything is ruled according to cosmic law, individual independence and the possibility of choice do not exist. None of the beings which reside in the cosmos can act at will; all are bound by cosmic law. When we die and return to the spiritual world, we too will follow cosmic law.

Freedom and choice have not always been absent from the cosmos. Long ago the cosmos was constantly changing, metamorphosing and evolving. However, in the course of its evolution the cosmos became rigid and inflexible. Progress came to a standstill. Rigidity became law; cosmic law became rigid. And as long as cosmic law remains rigid the further evolution of the universe will be impossible as well. Cosmic inflexibility will have to continue until new and free conditions can be established in the cosmos.

In order to establish these free cosmic circumstances extraordinary events took place. A new celestial being was conceived which would not be constrained by the limits of cosmic law. This new celestial being could not be fashioned in the cosmos because everything in the spiritual world—by cosmic law—must follow cosmic law. Entirely unique conditions had to be founded where the new celestial entity could develop and mature under conditions which were not restricted by rigid cosmic law. Therefore, a location outside the spiritual world was established where cosmic law would have no authority or power. This location outside the spiritual world is our solar system with the planet earth as the crown of its development. Man is the celestial being that was created to reside on the earth and assume the immense responsibility of creating independence for the cosmic world.

Man—who is a spiritual being—can live and develop for only a limited amount of time outside the region where cosmic law rules. This amount of time is LIFE ON EARTH. Only during life on earth are we exempt from cosmic law. The unbendable laws of the cosmos do not control or determine the course of a man's life and actions on earth. Before birth and after death, when we live in the spiritual world, we stringently have to follow cosmic law. We were given life on earth to establish independence for the spiritual world. However, man cannot be required to create freedom of choice. The contradiction inherent in this is obvious. The moment something is demanded from us, our decision concerning it cannot be free. Our task can be completed successfully only if—individually, of our own volition—we choose to create freedom of choice and through our decision, help to establish independence from cosmic law.

When mankind was put on the earth, however, the connection to his spiritual origin was not immediately severed. For a long period celestial cosmic beings attended to man on the earth in much the same way that parents choose to care for a baby. Then, when man reached a viable level of maturity, the support of the divine cosmic beings gradually was withdrawn so we could proceed towards accomplishing our task. Nonetheless, even during our life on earth we still need to reconnect with our cosmic origin in a daily rhythm. We do this in what we call sleep.

We can look at the Old Testament as a metaphor of this mission for mankind. In the Old Testament we find many examples of the fostering of man by divine beings. When we read its stories we can ask ourselves, does man already make his own decisions, or does he still feel bound by tradition? Does he dare to break away from cosmic law? The Old Testament narration of Adam and Eve is a beautiful illustration of this. In the Book of Genesis we are told about Adam and Eve and the Garden of Eden. Eve was tempted by the serpent to eat an apple from the forbidden tree and then offered it to Adam as well. As a result they were expelled from Paradise. This has come to be known as the "Fall of Man."

Yet, if we look at the story in light of what we have come to know about the true purpose for the creation of man, we see that Adam and Eve were confronted with a choice. A clear commandment from God had been given. But, these first earthly beings found themselves in a situation where they were able to choose whether or not to follow cosmic law, the law of God. It was

Eve who actively confronted and challenged cosmic law. Eve was the first human being to take up freedom of choice. Instead of cursing her for her deed we ought to make her our heroine.

Of course, the Old Testament is not usually interpreted in this way. Calling Eve our heroine may even seem foolish. However, if we consider the contents of the Old Testament from this unaccustomed perspective we may find that many of its stories take on new meaning. In reality these Old Testament stories are accounts of events which should teach mankind to become free beings, making their own way on the earth, independent of rigid cosmic law. These stories provide us with timeless examples that can inspire us to break away from traditional, familiar ways of thinking, to re-examine what we have been taught and what we believe. These stories continue to have validity for mankind, even today.

The question might arise: If we are spiritual beings—living on the earth by day, visiting our spiritual origin every night and returning to the spiritual world at death—why don't we have any recollection of our times in the world of the cosmos? Once again, we will find the answer is not complicated. We could not create independence from cosmic law if we always had to be mindful of the (cosmic) insights we acquire during our sojourns in the spiritual world between death and birth or during sleep. If we were continuously conscious of ourselves as spiritual beings, as well as the cosmic laws that govern the actions of spiritual beings, our ability to learn to make independent choices on earth would be severely hindered. We never would be able to accomplish our cosmic task. Therefore it was crucial that we lose conscious knowledge of our spiritual existence while we conduct our life on the earth.

Thousands of years ago mankind still had conscious knowledge of his cosmic origin. Moreover, everyone possessed an ongoing insight into the occurrences in the spiritual world through what is called clairvoyance. As a result of reaching a certain level of maturity mankind gradually had to lose this natural clairvoyance. With the disengagement of our clairvoyant faculties we also lost awareness that once we had been intimately connected with the spiritual world.

With increasing frequency we are encountering instances of a renewed consciousness of cosmic connections. As the beginning of the twenty-first century approaches we are reaching a stage in the evolution of mankind where clairvoyance is returning. This actually is a gradual process. At first only a few people will become clairvoyant. In the course of the next decades and centuries many more will have regained this faculty of insight into the spiritual world. It is profoundly important that we prepare ourselves to face the ramifications of this fact.

At present this new clairvoyance is emerging in many forms, among them channeling and past-life regression. However, clairvoyant indications come from sources residing in the cosmos which are bound by cosmic law and which have no regard for our task of developing freedom of choice. Therefore, we must be extremely cautious about information obtained from these new clairvoyants. Before we can make use of the information dispersed through these sources, we first must achieve some degree of freedom of choice in our own life. Our own freedom of choice will give us the necessary insight and autonomy to evaluate clairvoyant communications critically and then to decide consciously if we want to make use of them. In fact, people who have not yet reached a level of freedom of choice in their own lives can do nothing constructive with clairvoyant information. These people are easily lured into following the indications of a being in the spiritual world which itself obediently must follow cosmic law. Whatever their reaction, decisions in situations such as these are not the result of free choice.

Daily life provides us with a remarkable learning process. The events of daily life which compel us to make decisions and to take a stand are the means by which we should learn to attain freedom of choice.

III

MANIFESTATIONS OF EVIL

We live in a confusing, often bewildering world. Wherever we look we see fear, loneliness, aggression, poverty, injustice, disease. Positions of power and authority frequently are held by people undeserving of our respect or support. These situations seem to cry out for a reaction from us. Intuitively we want to fight for what is right and to challenge the falsehood we see in the world. From experience we know instant results don't exist. Yet we feel impatient with the lack of progress we see and demand immediate cures for the world's ills. At the same time we know there are no all encompassing answers to the problems we face in our own lives.

The reason we have been unable to discover satisfactory solutions is not because of any inadequacy of ours, but instead lies in the the way life's problems are presented to us. From childhood on we are told if something is not right it must be wrong. Everything is defined for us in terms of polarities: rich or poor, fat or thin, beautiful or ugly, success or failure. We are taught about the entire world in polarities. As a result of such statements we are lead away from the real issues. In fact, the reality of life is not to be found in polarities and extremes, but in equilibrium, the middle ground, the balance. Statements that try to explain life as a polarity are precisely what confuse us.

Life itself reveals the truth of this assertion in many ways. Observe a toddler learning to stand upright. Once he has pulled himself up on his feet, the job of standing has only just begun. He must find the balance between falling forward or backward, left of right. Adults may be amused by the sight of this wobbly baby, but the fact is, he is hard at work finding his balance and learning a basic truth of life. The way we maintain our body temperature is another example of equilibrium being the proper stance. We immediately know we are sick if our temperature falls to 94° F or rises to 104° F. But we are in good health when our temperature is maintained at a consistent 98.6° F. In the same way, when we drive a car we are as much a hazard going too slow as when we drive too fast. The correct approach to life, the truth always lies in the balance, in the middle, not in the polarities. Yet we are told constantly, in a thousand different ways, "If you are not this, then you must be that." Everyday, around the world, on radio and television, in newspapers, books and magazines, examples of this radical, unrealistic approach go undisputed and unchallenged. As a consequence, we have lost heart to even question statements like these in our own lives. If we are ever to succeed in our task we must dare to address this issue in a straightforward way. Only then will it become clear to us in our own lives and in what we do that the answers we need are found in the middle, the balance, not in the polarities.

The problems we face as a result of this thinking in polarities are particularly evident in the way evil manifests in the world. Evil presents us with only one face, which carries many names—among them the devil, Satan, Mephistopheles, the enemy. We are taught to believe that evil has only one, easily recognizable form. But from experience we sense that evil is more complicated than that. Where is the mistake, the distortion in our picture? We easily could conclude as a consequence of the way evil is described, if we are against evil we must be good. Of course, when we see it expressed in this simplistic way, the folly of such a conclusion is apparent immediately. If we dare to be honest about ourselves, we must admit we have too many mischievous qualities to believe we are good, just by taking a stand against evil. The way good and evil are presented to us creates our dilemma and confusion and leads away from the real issue.

To find the key to solving the dilemma of our perception of evil we must go back to the time mankind was given the task of creating independence from cosmic law. When mankind was given its mission, two high cosmic beings, Lucifer and Ahriman, were assigned to help mankind. The way these two cosmic entities lend support to mankind can best be compared with the way a coach trains his athletes. A good coach knows he can't go easy on his team. He must demand more of their strength and talents than they think they can give. The coach requires that they strive for the limit of their abilities and beyond. During training, his team may have grumbled and complained, frequently felt overtaxed and worn down. On occasion, the team members may have even wished him less than the best. Nonetheless, when his team wins, the coach is hailed and admired. Such a coach is considered to be a good one.

The function which Lucifer and Ahriman perform for mankind is similar to what a coach does for his team. Lucifer and Ahriman know that mankind was created and placed on the earth to establish freedom of choice. And they try to assist us in this task by creating the greatest resistance, just as the coach does with his players. When we reflect on the dilemmas and challenges we are faced with in daily life, we easily can see that Lucifer and Ahriman consider throwing us off balance as an outstanding achievement on their part. Lucifer and Ahriman will go to extremes, deliberately placing hindrances and hardship on our path in order to strengthen us for our mission. In this way, they test our ability to become competent and empowered to establish freedom of choice. Lucifer and Ahriman cannot give freedom of choice to us. We must win it through our deeds. But they help us by throwing us off balance, by confusing us in a thousand different ways, by creating opportunities for us to exercise our ability to make choices.

Lucifer tries to help us by tempting us in the direction of our spiritual origin. He does this by trying to persuade us that all experiences of earthly life are a waste of time, that the only reality exists in the spiritual world. He says, "Be good and devout. Pray and meditate. Never forget, not even for a moment, that your origin is in the cosmos. Do not pay any attention to the material world. Only the spiritual world is real and meaningful. Don't fall for the perversities of life on earth. Life in the spiritual world is beautiful beyond compare; in fact, there was really no need for you to incarnate. There is no way you can satisfactorily justify life on earth. In reality you are a spiritual being, and you would be much better off if you would just ignore the material world altogether." If we were to follow Lucifer's advice exclusively we would withdraw from the world, neglecting the responsibilities of life and our earthly task of creating freedom of choice.

Ahriman, on the other hand, wants us to think real life only takes place on earth. He tells us, "Life on earth is beautiful. You only live once. Live it to the fullest. This is the only life you're ever going to have, so you'd better get out there and enjoy it. Grab what you can. If you have to cheat to get what you want, go ahead. Do whatever it takes. Just don't get caught. Don't wait until you've grown up to have fun. Patience is for old folks with nothing better to do. There are quick and easy explanations for everything. You don't even have to give it much thought. Find a system, plug in your problems and crank out the solutions. Then you'll have even more time for the pleasures of life. If it feels good, do it. Have fun. Make love. That is the only reason why you are alive. Religion is for bloodless fools who don't dare to face life, who think there is a God. There is no spiritual world; that's an illusion. There is no judgement day, either. Live for today. When you die, you're dead." This is the approach Ahriman uses to challenge us and lure us away from our genuine task.

To make it even more confusing for us Lucifer and Ahriman disguise themselves so that it is extremely difficult to recognize them individually. However, there is one critical factor which can help us to identify them. Lucifer and Ahriman—as cosmic beings—are constrained by and inextricably bound to cosmic law. This key factor makes it possible for us to recognize their activity and influence in our lives. In fact, it is fundamental that we do so. If we identify the way they work and the manner in which they manifest in the world, we can also find ways to withstand them.

We can use the following example to demonstrate how they attempt to beguile us. We often hear that it doesn't matter if the earth is destroyed by nuclear explosions or devastated by pollution. There are those who would have us believe so many galaxies exist in the cosmos our earth wouldn't be missed at all. This makes as much sense as someone saying: "It doesn't matter if I cut out your heart. You weigh a hundred and fifty pounds, and your heart only weighs one pound. You still would be left with one hundred forty-nine pounds. What's a pound? You won't even miss it." The person who says this to you might be right. You won't notice that your heart is missing because with the removal of this one, seemingly unimportant pound your life will have been extinguished. Unfortunately, the person who told you this will discover the obvious and irreversible error in his logic only after he has destroyed your existence.

We regularly hear similar remarks made about the earth and other galaxies. We live on this planet. The other galaxies are billions of miles away and chances are none of us will ever be able to travel to any of them. Nor will we ever be able to inhabit any of those other galaxies. Doesn't it make more sense to pay attention to what takes place on earth, to stop nuclear and chemical devastation of this planet, than to look for our salvation in a scientific nightmare? Why is it that only a few people are willing to confront the issue and take a firm stand?

Consider the way intergalactic travel is presented in light of what we have said about the working of evil in the world. Then the source of such remarks suddenly becomes visible. These remarks about the other galaxies are influenced by Lucifer. In them we can see a perfect example of a Luciferic seduction. Lucifer tries to confuse and confound us with scientific-sounding information, and as a result we almost are convinced by his promises. At the same time he lures us into neglecting our genuine task of living life on earth and achieving freedom of choice. We begin to ponder the possibilities of travel to other galaxies and extra-terrestrial civilizations, of leaving behind the mess we have made of things on earth. We are lulled into forgetting that the earth is the most essential element of the cosmos, that we have been placed on earth to accomplish a momentous mission.

The manifestation of Lucifer and Ahriman constantly appear among us. True to their mission, Lucifer and Ahriman ceaselessly try to win us over to their views. We must find the courage to recognize the manifestation of these two beings and build up the inner strength to withstand their temptations and lures. The way we live, how we perform our duties, how we think and interact with others—these are the genuine avenues to freedom of choice.

During our life on earth, we must discover and maintain a balance between the enticements of Lucifer and Ahriman. While we live on earth we never must forget that our origin lies in the spiritual world. This is what Ahriman would like us to do. And Lucifer would be delighted if we would dream away about the spiritual world, forgetting that we have an earthly task. Mankind was created to accomplish a profoundly important mission on earth. There is no other being who can take up this mission, nor is there another domain in the universe where this goal can be accomplished. Only mankind and the earth are exempt of cosmic law.

In this way we progressively begin to comprehend that, although we perceive it as having only one face, in truth evil consists of two entities, Lucifer and Ahriman. Mankind must keep itself in balance between Ahriman and Lucifer who reveal themselves as one, but who are actually the polarities of evil. As a rule, it should be possible to maintain ourselves in equilibrium between two polarities. Yet, as long as these two evil entities are perceived as one this balance will be difficult for us to find. We need to recognize consciously the reason why evil is usually so difficult to distinguish in life. Ahriman and Lucifer know our task is to create freedom of choice on earth. They are delighted when they are able to confuse, perplex or embarrass us, leaving us incapable of discovering what is right and what is wrong. Only when we learn to recognize them and distinguish their disclosures in the events of the world will we be able to gain ground. It is up to us to persevere. We must be more true to our mission than they are to theirs.

Our appreciation of what it means to be alive will change entirely when we realize that mankind is the most crucial element in the universe. The implications of this realization are far-reaching. Many people contend that the cosmic world progresses regardless of what we do, and that our evolution is independent of the evolution of the cosmos. In fact, just the opposite is true. When mankind develops, our progress will give rise to the further evolution of the universe. The future of the cosmos is dependent on mankind. That is the reality. The development of mankind is essential to the continuing progress of the universe. We dare not assume that we can or should wait for the cosmos to show us what to do. The deeds of man determine the future of the cosmos. We have a tremendous and profound responsibility to care for the progress of the universe, the future of the earth, the evolution of mankind, and the moral and spiritual enlightenment of every human being, individually.

When we finally will have accomplished independence from cosmic law by our own free deeds—not because we were predestined to do so, but out of our own inner drive for freedom—the evolution of the universe will resume. Man will be the only spiritual entity to have this independence from cosmic law. Mankind will then guide the other spiritual beings in the cosmos in reaching self-determination. Only then will the universe be released from rigid cosmic law and give rise to a completely new and emancipated cosmos. In this new universe each spiritual being will have authority over its own activity, each will be responsible to itself. There will be no set conditions. Nothing will be pre-determined. Evil will have no part in this new universe. Ahriman and Lucifer will have fulfilled their task.

We must be conscious, however, that Ahriman and Lucifer are obligated here and now to make life on earth so arduous for us. Their assignment was not assumed of their free will; rather it was given to them as a mission when mankind was conceived. Only when we establish independence from cosmic law will Lucifer and Ahriman become free beings. They then will resume their original high rank in the spiritual world which they sacrificed in order to help mankind. Only then will they too no longer be bound by cosmic law. It is part of our responsibility to set free these two highly evolved spiritual beings that at present make our life so difficult. All this can lead us to only one momentous conclusion:

Man is the pivotal point in the evolution of the cosmos.

This, of course, sounds incredible. However, it should not be cause for arrogance or presumption on our part. If we are honest, we have to admit that, up to now, we have not made very good use of our potential. In fact, we have repeatedly allowed Lucifer or Ahriman to lead us astray. But it is not too late. We can still fulfill our mission.

When the whole picture is taken into account we will understand immediately that life is a possibility to grow, a challenge to gain strength for our task. Life on earth is granted us to help us on our path to creating and attaining freedom of choice. Many people regard life as a punishment, as something predestined and predetermined. That, of course, is just what Lucifer and Ahriman want. Instead of tackling the challenges in life, they want us to resign ourselves to whatever comes our way. They would be exceedingly pleased if we simply would fall for their lure.

We must constantly remind ourselves that cosmic independence will not be handed to us. We have to work intensively for it; we have to establish it through our own deeds. Lucifer and Ahriman can bring about situations in which we will be able to make choices, but they should not choose for us. In our time the challenges are greater than ever; disasters are in the making all around. This is where Ahriman steps in. His voice is all too familiar to many of us: "Why wait until you know what's going on? What you need is a quick fix, a quick answer. Don't wait to act. It doesn't matter what you do or how you do it. Just do something, anything—now."

We will only be able to make choices, to perform our duty properly, if consciously we know what we are doing, if we know what our goal is. We must not act without awareness of what in reality is demanded of us. We must know and evaluate before we act. We cannot evaluate if we do not correctly comprehend. Acting without thinking is exactly what Ahriman and Lucifer want us to do. It is our responsibility to learn to act out of a conscious perception of, and understanding for the consequences of our deeds. The way for us to achieve this is to have conscious knowledge of the world in which Lucifer and Ahriman must live and the cosmic laws they must follow.

IV

LIFE AFTER DEATH

We will better understand the influences of Lucifer and Ahriman on earthly life when we are acquainted with the laws that govern their actions, the laws of the cosmos. We already know that after death we return to the spiritual world and must follow cosmic laws once again. This fact is fundamental to our pursuit. There is much more that we can discover about death and the spiritual world.

An abundance of descriptions of life after death are available to us. They range in depth and scope from the ancient *Tibetan Book of the Dead* and the *Egyptian Book of the Dead* to the various explanations given by Buddhism, Judaism, Islam, and the Christian denominations. Each describes, in its own way, what happens to the human soul and spirit at death. Some of the nearly 350 books of writings and transcribed lectures by the Austrian philosopher Rudolf Steiner give vivid explanations of what the human being experiences after earthly death. The work of Raymond Moody and Elisabeth Kübler-Ross offer us a contemporary view of death. In Dr. Moody's book, *Life After Life* (1975), the death process is described breathtakingly and beautifully by people who have been reanimated after a near-death experience. These people relate that death began with a feeling of relief and profound bliss. They felt as if they were moving through a tunnel toward a majestic being of light. They also perceived a review of the events of their life.

Each of these descriptions leads us closer to a clearer understanding of how life on earth transforms into life in the spiritual realm. If we reflect on these descriptions we can discover a new understanding of the meaning of death and life. We will come to see that death is not the end of life. Death is the victory of spirit over matter. Death is rebirth into the spiritual world; it is returning home. In the cosmos death is regarded as a joyous, very beautiful, inspiring and perfect event. Remarkably, on earth we regard birth in the same way.

After death we experience the blissful moment of our birth back into the spiritual world. This moment stands in our memory as a beacon, a radiant guide post during our sojourn in the cosmos. Dr. Moody reports that many people who have died and are revived are resentful that they have been reanimated and brought back to life. Only with the greatest effort could they force themselves to break away from the glowing feeling of hominess they felt in the spiritual world and return to an earthly life. During their brief encounter with the spiritual world, some people learned the task for their life on earth and accepted a new challenge in life. Their fear of death disappeared; they came to know with certainty that life continues after they die.

At the moment of death we lay aside our physical body. Our ego, our eternal spiritual essence, begins its passage into the spiritual world. This journey home takes place in several stages over a long period. Although we exist in the spiritual world as a spiritual entity, for a long time our interest still remains bound up with the earthly world. During the period of bliss that accompanies our entry into the spiritual world after death we perceive our earthly deeds by way of a kind of imaginative perception. We witness the events of the life we have just completed passing before us in a lively, colorful panorama. No objective judgments are made about what we have done during life. Nor are feelings aroused in us about what we see passing in review. We simply are aware of the events of our life. This panorama and the experience of bliss have a duration of approximately three days, after which they gradually fade away.

After this episode of panorama, there is so much light and activity that we are unable to distinguish what is happening. We feel as though blinded by it, completely overwhelmed by everything that is taking place around us. On earth we have a similar experience when we drive a car through a long, dark tunnel and abruptly emerge into bright daylight. Instead of seeing, we are blinded by the blazing light. Only gradually do we adapt to our brilliant surroundings and regain our bearing. Much the same thing happens when we die; we adapt only gradually to our new and unfamiliar spiritual surrounding.

We then enter a setting in the spiritual world which is designated by the Sanskrit word kamaloka, or "region of desire." It must be understood from the outset that kamaloka is not a location but rather a state of existence, like childhood or old age. In kamaloka we are still bound by our interest in the deeds we performed on earth. As we gradually adapt to kamaloka we encounter several experiences simultaneously that can best be described separately. Each experience affords us an opportunity to face the result of the way we lived our life on earth.

The first is related to the desires, yearnings, cravings and lusts we had on earth. As an example of what we will all undergo in kamaloka let us imagine someone who had an exaggerated or immoderate habit, like chain smoking. Think of the kind of person who—even before he gets out of bed—feverishly searches for his cigarettes and lighter; the one who only feels alive again after the first inhaled draw. When he dies he leaves his physical body behind on earth. However, even though cravings and desires are the result of earthly experiences, they are carried over into the spiritual realm. When this chain-smoker regains his bearing after encountering the overwhelming light in the spiritual world his first thoughts are: "Where are my cigarettes? Where is my lighter?" His physical body, his cigarettes and his lighter were cast off at the moment of death, but the frame of mind associated with his smoking habit remain with him. He is conscious of his desperate need for that first inhaled draw. He longs to satisfy his craving for a cigarette. His desire grows ever stronger and more intense. Unfortunately there is no way for him to fulfill his agonizing yearning. In kamaloka all he can do is endure the tortuous thoughts he has about them.

During kamaloka, the next phase in our return to the spiritual world, we burn off our earthly habits and dissociate from them, whatever they might have been: smoking, drinking, gossiping, eating in excess, sex. Of course, some of these activities are essential for life. However, immoderate, excessive cravings satisfy more than our needs. Our habits, cravings and lusts linger with us in the cosmic world but cannot be satisfied. We must go through the agony of longing, desiring and wanting, without being able to satisfy these feelings. Tormented by our exaggerated cravings, we will dwell in kamaloka until they have been burnt off and dissolved.

The longings and habits we were unwilling or unable to overcome during our life on earth become our obsessions and fixations during kamaloka. In this phase we feel the urgent need to correct those exaggerated desires which we could not bring under control on earth. However, by cosmic law in the spiritual world, we can resolve to change, but we cannot make a change. Only while we live on earth in a physical body are we able to perform deeds and acts. It is vastly important for us to be aware that the task of transforming our vices into virtues can be accomplished only during life on earth. When we reincarnate we are given the opportunity to put these virtues to use as part of our character.

During kamaloka, in addition to the ordeal of burning off our earthly cravings and desires, we simultaneously experience the recapitulation of our past earth life. This recapitulation takes place in reverse sequence, on two different levels at the same time. On one level we experience the events of our life in reverse order, beginning with the moment of our recent death and ending at the moment of our birth on earth. The second reversal has to do with feelings experienced during our lifetime. During our sojourn in kamaloka, we do not experience and feel what we ourselves have felt or endured as result of our deeds and thoughts. In kamaloka we feel and experience what others have felt and sensed as a result of our thoughts and deeds. During our life on earth we have many thoughts and perform innumerable deeds, all of which influence others. For example, consider what happens to someone who causes a serious auto accident. While this person is driving his car far in excess of the speed limit, another car suddenly crosses his path. The first person is unable to avoid a collision. The driver of the second car is mortally wounded and dies. When years later the speeding driver meets his own death he must relive this accident in kamaloka. In kamaloka, however, he feels the events, the shock and the pain entirely as the other driver and his family did. The speeding driver will have to live with this pain and anguish for the duration of his sojourn in kamaloka. He is unable to push out of his thoughts the feelings and suffering of the second driver, his family and friends—as he might have been able to do on earth. He must live with this emotional awareness; it becomes part of the reality of his spiritual existence. He has no choice but to live with the painful truth of this situation. There is no escaping it. He faces the harsh reality that truth and cosmic law rule in the spiritual world. On earth we could have pulled a veil of shame over any deed we did not want to remember. In the spiritual world there are no such veils. If we are ashamed in the spiritual world, we cannot evade the feelings shame evokes in us. We are tormented and harassed by this shame as long as we are in kamaloka. As a result we decide that we want to make up for the suffering we inflicted on others. We feel the resolve to heal the mistakes of the past, but we cannot act on this decision while we are in the spiritual world. In order to act we must return to the only stage on which we can perform deeds, the earth. And so, after a long time in kamaloka and the cosmos, we resolve to return to earth to make up for our actions in our previous incarnation, and to continue on our upwardly evolving path.

We should not conclude from this that the purpose of life on earth in a new incarnation is only repentance. Life should be regarded as a new chance, a challenge, not as punishment. We know from experience that results can be achieved only through effort. Whatever problems arise during life, they come our way to be solved, to challenge us to be stronger, not as a punishment for past mistakes. An excellent illustration of such effort can be seen when we watch a baby chick struggling to hatch from its egg. Its labor and perseverance are an amazing and inspiring illustration of this point. At first, only a tiny crack appears in the thick and leathery egg shell. Later, a minute opening appears and the chick becomes visible. The chick wrestles to break away part of the shell with its beak in order to create a passage large enough to allow it to escape its confinement. In the end it frees itself and collapses, wet and totally exhausted. It may remain in this condition for nearly two hours. Then it will pull itself together and start to walk. While we observe this miracle, we may feel an overwhelming urge to help the baby chick by making the crack a little bit larger, or opening the shell so that it may more easily escape. However, such intervention would cause the chick's death. It needs the struggle to be capable of not only starting life, but surviving as well. It needs this challenge, this struggle, so that it can build up and strengthen its forces.

The same principle holds true when a boxer signs to fight a match. He doesn't conserve his energy by staying in bed during the weeks before the fight. He seeks out sparring partners who will vigorously oppose him and challenge his skills, so that he can build up the forces he will need to be victorious in the ring.

What is valid for a baby chick or for a boxer is valid for all of us. Through opposition we grow stronger. Only through facing and overcoming obstacles do we develop and mature. Life presents challenges for this reason. Each of us must decide for ourselves how to utilize these challenges to our best advantage.

These ideas may give rise to some intriguing questions. "We lived former lives on earth. In our past incarnation we were probably assertive, responsible adults who cared about the world and others. Why then are we reborn as babies? Why must we struggle for such a long time before we are grown-up once again? If we were reliable and respected adults in our former incarnation, why do we come back so helpless and inexperienced? Wouldn't it make more sense if we were required by cosmic law to return as adults, so we could get right to work?" If we put to use what we have learned already about the spiritual nature of mankind, the answer to these questions can be found without much difficulty.

Suppose you had been Cleopatra in your former incarnation. Wouldn't it be exceedingly pleasant to return in your next life with all the beauty, wisdom and wealth you possessed in the former one? Just imagine what it would be like for Cleopatra to return today in a new incarnation with all the beauty, wisdom and wealth of her former incarnation. She would find that the world was no longer like it was when she ruled Egypt. She would be faced with airplanes, computers, TV, microwaves. Modern life would be incomprehensible to her. Cleopatra would be overwhelmed by the fascination of modern technology and all her energy would be spent trying to cope with these curious and unfamiliar devices. They most probably would drive her insane. The reasons she had decided to reincarnate and what she had intended to achieve in her new incarnation would be lost in the confusion.

In fact, were we to return to life as an adult we would continue in this incarnation exactly where we left off in the previous one. It would be as if we had learned nothing from the lessons of the previous life, as if our life would resume without having gone through the lessons of kamaloka. During kamaloka we recapitulate the deeds of our previous life. We examine our conduct, undergo for ourselves the effects they had on others, and learn from them. As a result of the insight gained during kamaloka we decide to come back in a new incarnation. When we return to earth for a new life we live in a different era, in new surroundings, unlike those we lived in before. We need to adapt to these new and different circumstances; we have to learn about the changes the world has undergone during our absence and acquire the skills to survive. We learn to adjust to the new environment and not to be stunned by all the new developments only because we return as babies.

At this stage in our discussions we need to look at another facet of the composition of our spiritual being. Our spirit or ego (our eternal part) directs us from incarnation to incarnation. Our ego grows, changes and modifies according to what it experienced during life on earth and as the results of kamaloka. However, the ego—or spirit—on its own cannot experience anything earthly. For this the ego needs an interpreter which is the soul. The spirit unites with the soul before birth and this union continues through life on earth into life after death. On earth the soul receives the impressions of the outside world and translates them for the ego into emotions and feelings. After death the soul and spirit remain united until the soul has imparted all the impressions that were imprinted on it during life to the spirit. Even during its sojourn in kamaloka the spirit still needs the soul to interpret the experiences it undergoes. At the conclusion of kamaloka the soul's task will be fulfilled; it has communicated all of its earthly and spiritual impressions to the spirit. The spirit will no longer need the soul's assistance, and spirit and soul separate.

The distinction between soul and spirit can best be explained by a picture. When a drop of sea water is thrown back into the sea, it merges with the substance of the sea and can no longer be found as an individual drop. In the same way the soul reverts to the soul-world after kamaloka. The soul blends with the soul-substance of the cosmos. This holds true for the soul but not for the spirit. The spirit (or ego) is a UNIQUE, ETERNAL INDIVIDUALITY which goes from incarnation to incarnation.

During our former incarnation and during kamaloka our spirit perceived through the soul all the impressions of the recent life on earth. During and after each incarnation the spirit is imprinted with the essence of the consequences of all the experiences of life on earth. As a result the spirit is transformed, modified, perfected. Our spirit was dissimilar in past incarnations from the way it is now. Through the transformations and the process of perfection the spirit endures, it carries the harvest of the former earthly life into the next incarnation. Cause and justification for the course of our present life lie hidden in our previous incarnations. What we experience in this life are the modified consequences of our former incarnations. The life we live today is an outcome of the events we created in our previous lives.

We share the time in kamaloka with many souls—we speak of soul during kamaloka for practical reasons; in reality we should state: spirit united with soul. We congregate with the souls of the people we met during our past life on earth. During our sojourn in kamaloka, we reconnect with each and every human being we were associated with on earth. However, life in the spiritual world is distinctly different from life on earth. On earth no one knows what we think or feel unless we want them to know. Our thoughts are our own; no other being has access to them. This is not the case in the spiritual world. In the spiritual world, what we think and feel is manifested externally. We cannot hide who we are nor what we feel; in the spiritual world—where only cosmic law rules—there is no concealment, pretense or deceit. When we meet other beings in the cosmos we are able to communicate with them in a sort of mutual—spiritual—interpenetration. We converse in a way which is similar to having meaningful eye contact with someone on earth. There are actually no words to describe this. What we think, they think; what we feel, they feel. The other being is susceptible to our innermost affections. We mirror or reflect one another. If we were friends on earth this meeting in the world of the spirit is an incredible experience, reassuring, close and warm. It is unforgettable and makes an everlasting impression on us, which we always long to recapture.

In the spiritual world we could also encounter a soul who led an extremely vicious and evil life on earth, someone we would not want to meet in a dark alley. Since we are in the spiritual world, this being must try to mirror us in order to communicate with us. Even though he is a wicked soul he wants to reflect good souls. He is not at all attracted to other vicious souls. He does not like their appearance, nor the viciousness emanating from them. He wants to be understood, to feel what good souls feel and to mirror their spiritual image. He attempts to communicate with us and to reflect our emotions. Since he is an evil soul he is unable to mirror who we are and cannot have these reassuring perceptions. He is disappointed in his failure with us, but nevertheless makes a new attempt. He is unsuccessful again. After several attempts he gives up and tries to connect with another soul. Of course, if that soul is also a good one, he will face the same difficulties. He will come to realize that he cannot commune with good souls; this will be difficult for him to bear. He would like very much to radiate the same goodness that others souls display. But since—by cosmic law—only truth rules in the spiritual world, he cannot achieve this. All his efforts fail. He feels abandoned and alone. However, even wicked souls need communion with others. Therefore, he will persist in making new attempts to associate with the souls around him until he finds one with whom he can create this mirrored reflection. What he then experiences is not to his liking. The soul he is able to reflect radiates wickedness and evil. Disgusted by the hideous features of this other soul, he turns away. He tries yet again with other souls and, of course, meets identical difficulties. The only souls he can communicate with, the only souls he can mirror, are wicked and evil. Gradually it dawns on him that he himself must be wicked and evil, too. This is a devastating discovery. The revelation of this truth hits hard. He lives in the spiritual world—the world of rigid cosmic law and truth—and this disclosure pierces the most profound depth of his being. He cannot escape the logical consequences of this discovery or the devastating thoughts it arouses in him. From these experiences he must learn his lesson and decide to become good so that when he returns to the earth for a next incarnation he will be able to make up for the evil he had perpetrated. He must try to heal the wounds he inflicted on those he met in former incarnations.

When someone has lived an exceedingly evil life on earth, caused harm to thousands, taken pity on no one, and sought revenge for whatever happened to him, such a soul will need a much longer time in kamaloka to endure the consequences of all the harm he caused. He cannot leave kamaloka before he has himself suffered all the pains, distress, grief, despair and hurt he has inflicted on each individual he met on earth. For example, if someone has worked with the death squadrons in South America and tortured countless people, he will have to endure kamaloka until he has gone through the consequences of every single one of his deeds. Such an evil soul could sojourn in kamaloka for nearly an eternity.

The consequences of our earthly actions are unavoidable. In kamaloka we see what we did on earth. We also see what we left unfinished. It is fortunate for us that cosmic law only rules in the cosmos. In the spiritual world we are aware of every characteristic of each soul we encounter. We are also thoroughly conscious of ourselves. If—while living on earth—we were forced to see our own ego and the ego of others in the same manner, the consequences of our perception would relentlessly obsess and haunt us. We would be paralyzed and unable to act. We would not be able to fulfill the task of creating freedom of choice. Therefore, during the time we live on earth and while we are becoming the being who will help create freedom of choice for the cosmos, the spiritual world veils our ego from us. If we were able to see our own ego we would be overcome by shame. If we were to reveal our ego to others we would find ourselves constantly in the most difficult and awkward situations. And yet, evil is a part of our life on earth. Wickedness is necessary to learn freedom of choice.

In kamaloka we meet the consequences of our past life. If we were good on earth, have cared about others, had sympathy and compassion, shared the joys and sufferings of friends, then our tenure in kamaloka will take approximately one third the number of years we lived on earth. If we die at the age of ninety, the time we need to spend in kamaloka will be approximately thirty years. When we have completed the state of kamaloka, we continue our sojourn in higher regions of the universe.

We are free of all earthly wants, desires, longings when we have passed through kamaloka. All the experiences of our past life have imprinted on our eternal spirit. Our soul is left behind in the soul-world in the same way that we left our physical body behind at death. We now proceed—as spirit only—into a different spiritual state of existence called devachan. The duration of devachan is much longer than kamaloka. During devachan we turn our attention away from our previous earth life. We no longer yearn for earthly experiences. Earthly thoughts and ideas were left behind in kamaloka. We communicate with other spiritual beings and lead a warm social existence in devachan. Nowhere in the spiritual world do we have a greater feeling of security and contentment than devachan. Once more, we must be aware of the difficulty of describing in words these spiritual encounters. In devachan we converse and communicate with the spirits of people we have known on earth as well as with spiritual beings who do not incarnate. We are nurtured by these encounters and feel closely connected with those we meet. Each meeting enriches us. Evil does not exist in devachan. We have only have the most elevated, spiritual contemplations and reflections.

After an extended period of social contact during devachan, we reach a condition of fulfillment. We wish to be on our own, to reflect on all of our spiritual encounters. We withdraw into ourselves. Eventually, we again feel the need to be together with other spiritual beings and return to the social ambience of devachan. Our existence in devachan continues to alternate between these social periods and periods of isolated contemplation. Initially the need for social contact outweighs the urge to reflect in solitude, so we spend a rather longer period communicating with others. Gradually our need to reflect and be on our own increases. As our stay in devachan progresses we come to recognize that our social contacts no longer nurture us. The yearning awakens in us to return to the earth and once more participate in the evolution of mankind. This precipitates the process of entering into a new earth life. We begin to contemplate a next incarnation and prepare for it. This new incarnation is like a memory of the future; it is the fulfillment of the resolve we made during devachan. This memory was the result of our struggles in the spiritual world; the realization of this resolve must be—indeed, can only be—accomplished on earth.

Although our ego is veiled, there are many ways our ego finds expression during life on earth. Our temperament in this life is the reflection of what we made of ourselves in former incarnations. This is what the mothers we spoke of earlier perceive in their babies before birth and what can be observed after they have been born. During life on earth we can alter the constitution of our character and temperament. This process of change is neither easy nor quick. But if we honestly try, we can change our temperament during life. Imagine if everyone had the same fits and outbursts of temper they had as a small child. If change were not possible for each and every one of us disaster would lurk around every corner.

We can achieve a change in our character only by pushing ourselves to the limits of our self-knowledge and beyond. Ask someone who smokes or drinks how much effort it takes to give up one of these habits acquired during life on earth. Perhaps this will help us to understand the tremendous effort it takes to change a character trait with which we were born, a character trait which we created by our actions in a former incarnation. Sometimes we meet older people who remind us of the wise, old grandmothers in fairy tales. They possess great understanding and profound wisdom. When asked, they will almost without exception explain that wisdom and knowledge were not always a part of their character. It took them a lifetime of struggle and effort to achieve the kind of knowledge that could be transformed into wisdom.

We must learn to appreciate the significance of the fact that only during life on earth can we reform our character. After death—in the spiritual world—we can see what we achieved or where we were unsuccessful. But after death we can no longer act. It is essential that we strive to improve our character during life on earth. The earth is the only place we can do so.

V

KARMA

What we created in one life serves as a seed for the next one. We call this seed karma. It should be made clear from the outset that karma and predestination are not the same. Karma can be transformed and shaped through our actions. Karma brings about situations which prompt us to make choices. The consequences of karma are not inevitable. We are entirely free to make choices in karmic situations. Predestination, on the other hand, is fixed and cannot be altered. We are predestined to confront the situation which karma brings us. From then on it is our free choice that determines the outcome. There is a widespread misconception that the results of karma are already written in the stars and that we are unable to influence their outcome. In this misrepresentation of the reality of karma we can detect Ahriman at work. Ahriman knows that if he can convince us that the resolution of karma is already predestined, our ability to face the consequences of karma and draw free conclusions will be paralyzed. As a result, we will not come to freedom of choice. He then will have succeeded in interfering with our task and our future.

During kamaloka we meet the souls of people with whom we were connected during life and we encounter the results of every situation we participated in on earth. We become aware of our accomplishments and failures, and the impact we had on others. We are conscious of each detail but during kamaloka we cannot act to change or correct anything. We recognize all that has happened—both good and bad—during our life but we cannot repair the harm we inflicted. This burdens our conscience. We are tormented by the discovery that we cannot correct our mistakes. A moment then arises when we understand we cannot act as long as we reside in the spiritual world. This leads us to decide to return to earth to make up for the shortcomings of our previous incarnation. From then on, our resolve and our desire to heal the past guide our spirit during its further sojourn in the spiritual world. This resolve, this determination is what we call karma. Karma is our design for the future, a master plan of our intentions to rectify our past. Karma is the plan for all further incarnations. Through the deeds we perform during this life we fashion the karma of our next incarnation. Karma is the memory of the future.

When we return to earth it is our karma that guides our actions. When we are born we lose conscious recollection of all our thoughts in the cosmos. However, the subconscious memory of our resolutions in kamaloka—our karma—accompanies us during this new incarnation. At the same time, karma leaves us free to follow or ignore the decisions we made in the spiritual world. The broad outline of our life, the condition of the physical body we inhabit, the place where we are born are all part of the karma we planned for ourselves. Karma also guides us intuitively to people with whom we must reconnect. We maneuver ourselves into situations where we will meet the same people—in their new incarnation, too—and have the possibility of re-establishing our previous relationships. This is one of life's preeminent joys and, at the same time, one of its greatest enigmas. Undoubtedly each of us has had such encounters or meetings more than once in life. Some parents have this feeling when they see their baby at the moment of birth. There is an immediate recognition, the feeling of being reunited at last. Other people describe having similar impressions when they met their spouse-to-be. They instantly knew this was the person they had been waiting for all their life. In the events that follow such meetings we sense there is a task that we must accomplish together; yet, as a rule, we are unaware of the underlying reasons for it. Ideally, we are able to work together to heal the mistakes and build upon the accomplishments of our shared past. If we carry out the resolutions we made in the spiritual world we bring our karma a bit nearer perfection.

People who are very earth-bound and materialistic in the way they approach life have lost all curiosity about how such encounters come to be. If they were only more inquisitive, they would find these meetings are not accidental. Such occurrences are not pure chance. These meetings are predestined. Every time we hear about such a meeting, or when we experience such a crucial meeting ourselves, only one remark is justified: life is stranger than fiction. The meetings we have are predestined; their outcome is not. Karma grants us the freedom to choose our response to every situation. This freedom gives each decision its own unique quality. The choice is ours to make when we begin a relationship, either personally or in business. We should be aware that we have the freedom to choose when a relationship is at an end, as well. Karma brings us together; it is our free choice to proceed as we see fit. We are free to decide our reaction to every situation life presents.

When we meet someone again in a new incarnation we hope we will be able to solve our past problems. However, meetings and situations can develop out of karma which do not heal the past. Circumstances may arise that are similar to those in our former incarnation. Imagine that during one life we were so disgusted with someone that we never again wanted anything to do with him. During kamaloka we realized that we ought to reconcile with this person and we made the decision to settle our differences. We knew in order to accomplish this we would have to meet again in our next incarnation. But when we actually meet we are unable to overcome our original feelings of disgust. As a result, we do not resolve our controversy. Therefore when we return once more to kamaloka, we will have to relive the same experience and recreate the resolve to reconcile. In our subsequent incarnation we again must try to set aside our differences with this person. In this way we are given the opportunity to work on the areas of our character that need improvement.

Through life we continue the learning process which moves us closer to the perfection of our character and the fulfillment of the mission of mankind. We can get a sense for the slowness of this learning process when we attempt to learn to play a musical instrument. In spite of our good intentions we have to stumble through our mistakes. With self-discipline and guidance, however, we ultimately master each new lesson. Every new incarnation involves such a learning process. If we are persistent we can improve ourselves with each successive life. However, we will continually falter on our path until we learn to understand the rules and principles that govern life. Through insight into these principles, we can learn to fulfill more quickly and creatively the purpose of earthly life. Patience for what comes our way and a refreshing understanding of life will then emerge. Life will begin to make sense.

We are connected during our life to the lives of thousands of others through encounters in our personal life as well as in our work. We are associated with each of these people for a reason. From what we have learned thus far, we know that the meeting with each person is predestined; the outcome is not. Even with karmic encounters, we are free to respond as we wish.

All of us have had the experience that someone of our acquaintance commands our attention and intrigues us more than other people. We one day realize that this person has become a good and trusted friend and a new dimension has been added to the relationship. We love this person. But what is love and where does it come from? An answer to this age-old question can be found in what occurs during our existence in the cosmos. We already know that in the spiritual world we recognize those souls with whom we were acquainted during earthly life. We communicate with them without words through a sort of spiritual interpenetration, similar to making eye-contact with someone on earth. We perceive the feelings we arouse in the soul we meet. In turn, the warmth the other radiates makes us glow. The kindness and sympathy the other emanates fill us with grace. We treasure each moment of contact. It is a quintessential feeling of benevolence and unparalleled completeness. Our spiritual sojourn is filled with countless radiant relationships and joyous sensations.

When we return to the earth in a new incarnation, we meet those with whom we have been together in a former life and in the spiritual world. The karma we have in common draws us together once again. These meetings need not occur only in our younger years. For numerous reasons many years may pass before our meeting actually takes place. However, when finally we meet these old acquaintances we have the impression of immediate recognition. We are overwhelmed by an awareness of having known one another before. This is one of the most glorious phenomenon we can experience in life. When we meet someone and from the first moment we realize "this is special," it fills us with a warm inner glow, great joy, and immense relief. Inwardly we know we are being reunited with someone for whom we have long waited. In fact we are experiencing a memory of the relationship we had with this person in the spiritual world. We call some of these encounters "love at first sight." However, the person we meet need not become our spouse. These connections can take many forms, but always give the feeling that they are a continuation of an enduring friendship. This is the true foundation of love. These encounters are among the most significant events we experience in our earthly life. Each human meeting denotes a connection to a previous incarnation. With these people we do not have to worry about what we say or do, or that we will be misunderstood. We can bare our innermost feelings and know we are perfectly safe. These karmic connections are a source of encouragement and offer a feeling of hominess. By their mere presence these people magnify the joys we experience in life. Because of the intimacy of the connection, they are able to console even our deepest sorrows and pains. We must understand that these karmic meetings happen to all of us and can have the most profound effect on our life and our future. If we are not alert, however, they can pass by unobserved. We should be grateful for every encounter with another person that stirs these feelings of recognition in us. Do we allow such an extraordinary meeting to pass by? Or do we freely take up the threads of the old relationship and weave them into the fabric of a new friendship for the future? Rightly understood, these feelings can reawaken our awareness of the reality of our spiritual origin.

VI

THE DOUBLE

It would be ideal if all relationships during life were as loving and kind as those portrayed in the previous chapter. However, we know this is simply not the case. Evil exists in the world and, to a lesser or greater degree, in each of us. What happens to someone who has been evil and harmful to others while on earth? How do the misdeeds and harm we have caused others effect us in the spiritual world?

We are usually not conscious of the fact that every deed is engraved in our memory, that each accomplishment leaves an imprint on our soul and that we carry this memory with us during life. The record of our actions engraved on our soul is concealed from our ordinary perception. If this were not the case, the nagging recollection of each act, every grand deed and insignificant gesture, would block our development and keep us from going on with life. Think, for example, of how we learn to write or play a musical instrument. If we were always reminded of the effort it took to master holding a pen and shaping the letters or learning the notes, we could never take another step. As soon as we have overcome the difficulty of a specific task we forget how much trouble it gave us. When we have passed one hurdle we forget the effort it required and proceed to the next one. Although the efforts are forgotten, we could recall them if we wished. It is obvious that they are stored somewhere inside us. In fact they are accumulated as marks on our soul. Our soul never forgets anything. These marks are invisible to our physical eye, but they are there, nevertheless. If we had eyes to see the invisible we would find on our soul the imprints of our evil deeds. We would see them as scars, stains and deformities.

When we enter the spiritual world after death, these invisible marks on our soul become spiritually discernable. In the spiritual world—where only truth rules—we see each stain, every scar and every deformity etched on our soul. The marks and scars are apparent to us as well as to other souls. There is no possibility of growth at the site of a physical scar. The same is true for scars imprinted on the soul. These scars are discernable as deformities on our soul and cannot be shed. These deformities and scars remain even as we progress further into the spiritual world. They are preserved for our next incarnation. This is true for every human being. When the time comes to reincarnate, these same scars and deformities reappear on our soul. However, now they do not appear only as scars. They manifest as cavities of varying shapes and sizes in the soul. They are voids and indentations where our soul can neither enter nor have power to rule. We are not conscious of these indentations. These cavities offer refuge and a comfortable residence in which other spiritual entities can live. There are countless beings in the spiritual world which cannot incarnate, but which would like to have an earthly dwelling for themselves. Beings of an ahrimanic nature find these voids attractive and they infiltrate them at once. This already occurs before birth. Ahrimanic entities cannot create a physical body; they must establish themselves in suitable places left open by someone else. These shelters will be their habitat until we die. These ahrimanic beings accompany every human being during life on earth. At death they must vacate their dwelling because ahrimanic beings cannot go through death. From what we have already learned, the mere thought that such ahrimanic entities live in us should be enough to make us shiver.

The grip such ahrimanic entities may have on a human being is described in literature in Oscar Wilde's *The Picture of Dorian Gray*, in Robert Louis Stevenson's *Dr. Jaeckel and Mr. Hyde*, in Tolstoy's *The Death of Ivan Ilyitch*, and in Dostojevsky's *The Double*. The name "double" which Dostojevsky gave to the sum total of these beings, is one we can easily use. These entities—which live in and off the soul of their host—duplicate, or double the soul of their host. The soul along with the double form an integrated totality; the double has access to those areas of the soul that the soul itself cannot occupy. The double has authority over these soul cavities, and tries to gain control of the soul's activity through its occupation of these spaces. This double lives as a parasite on and in the soul of every human being.

In a manner of speaking, the double is the manifestation of the wrongful actions of our former incarnations. The more cavities created in the soul as a result of evil deeds, the stronger the grasp these ahrimanic beings may have on the soul. The double tries to capture the greatest possible command over our soul.

From another angle, the double can be viewed as the reflected image of our karma. The double puts obstacles on our path for us to surmount. These obstacles serve as a reminder of the karma we have yet to fulfill. We know that the double is the manifestation of the evil deeds of our past. Karma is the expression of what we must still fulfill to remedy the evil deeds of our former incarnations. Karma and the double are two facets of the same principle; the double provides us a glimpse backwards at the deeds of our past life and the causes of our problems in this life. Karma is a glance forward, examining the deeds we still have to fulfill to release the double. When we work on our karma, we modify the cavities in our soul and diminish the command the double may have over us.

If the double becomes stronger than our ego and overpowers our ego, we may become a puppet for the double. We would then have to satisfy all of its evil wishes and cravings. We encounter a shocking and appalling manifestation of this in people who are addicted to alcohol or drugs. The double has taken over the reigns. We see them completely lose their dignity and moral sense. The reality is utterly frightening. And when someone is terrified he becomes paralyzed by fear. Through paralysis by fear they are an easy victim for the double who wants to enslave us and threaten our existence as honest and virtuous human beings. We must learn how to withstand the forces the double exerts from within. We must learn how to offset and counterbalance its dominance over our life.

There is only one remedy against this fear and enslavement by the double. We must learn how to offset and counterbalance its influence on our life. We can do this in many ways, among them acquiring inner strength through specific meditative exercises and living a life which makes us less vulnerable to the attacks of the double. We call such a lifestyle moral and honest. We can ward off the effects of the double if we strengthen ourselves spiritually. This is a conscious goal which can be achieved when we pursue a path of inner development. Such a path can lead us to discover one of the main laws of the cosmos as it affects life on earth: the deeds of one life have their consequences in the next incarnation. What we experience during this lifetime had its cause in our former lives. Or more dramatically: nothing in life is free, although the settlement of the debt is postponed until a subsequent incarnation. This, in its simplest form, is the law of karma. When we are able to understand this law which governs all human life on earth, life can be more fascinating and interesting. At the same time we will find it to be more complicated and complex. When we become aware of the laws that govern life, no two days will ever be the same. Life definitely will not be boring.

VII

THE ORIGIN OF RELIGION

We will gain an appreciation for a modern, Western path of spiritual development if we first examine the specific role of religion in the evolution of human consciousness. In our culture, we traditionally think of spiritual development in connection with church and religion.

What is religion? *The New Webster's Dictionary of the English Language* says "Religion; . . . origin uncertain . . . Recognition on the part of man of a controlling superhuman power entitled to obedience, reverence, and worship. . . ." This definition offers no help in understanding the significance of religion or the meaning of life.

We cannot imagine life without some form of religion. Religion has an immense impact on our daily lives. Preachers can be seen on television around the clock. There is an ongoing debate concerning the place of religion in government and in education. Religious wars rage around the globe and fill the headlines of our newspapers. Practically every nation in the world has an ambassador to the Vatican in Rome.

Has it always been like this? Most definitely not. Two thousand years ago Christianity evolved out of Judaism. We encounter the first manifestations of religion around 5,000 BC, in a region we nowadays designate as India. When we go back before 5,000 BC, there are no records among the ancient civilizations of anything which can be related even vaguely to religion. The oldest civilizations of which we have knowledge are the Chinese societies from around 20,000 to 10,000 BC. They had a highly cultured refinement and perfection in art, but we cannot find any indication of religion. They did not have religion. They did not need religion.

In our time, when we are deluged by religion, this is not an idea that we can easily comprehend. How can we grasp the fact that in ancient China there was no purpose or function for religion? The way to find the answer is to look again at the word religion. Although the dictionary says "origin uncertain," in reality the word religion reveals its meaning in its very makeup. We can cut the word in two: re-ligion. Re-ligion literally means to re-align, to re-connect. It is that easy. Religion seeks to enable us to come into contact again with the spiritual world, to re-unite with God. The truth of this is immediately apparent. The word religion indicates that man wants to realign and to reconnect with his spiritual origin.

Why then does the dictionary claim that the origin is unknown? Because in our time the idea that man descended from God and the spiritual world is no longer accepted. Today we have been lead to believe that man is the naked ape, the crown of Darwinian evolution. When we endorse the idea that man ascended from the animals, then we have to accept the full consequence of this thought. We must further assert that man originated on earth as a single cell at the moment of the Big-Bang and had to ascend the evolutionary ladder to his present stage. There is no God in the Darwinian theory of evolution; re-connecting with God makes no sense if we believe in the Darwinian metamorphosis.

When we direct our thoughts again to the China of 20,000 to 15,000 years ago, we must ask ourselves once more why they had no religion. There was no need for re-ligion, no need to re-align with the world of the spirits in old China. At that time man was still connected to the world out of which he had originated. Each human being was clairvoyant. Every human being still had his own connection with the spiritual world. Each person knew first-hand what was going on in that realm. In those times each human being had prophetic premonitions. Mankind had only recently descended from the cosmos; the human being was connected by a kind of spiritual umbilical cord to its origin. Only after man had matured enough and had completed its embryonic stage on earth was the umbilical cord cut.

In China of 20,000 years ago people were aware of their spiritual origin. Both their origin and the spiritual world were tangible truth to them. They had just come to earth. For the most part they were still spiritual beings which had taken on earthly characteristics only to a small extent. They remembered cosmic law and conducted their lives on earth in much the same way they had in the cosmos. In the course of evolution they gradually became more earth-man, less cosmic being. In this process of growing away from the cosmos, mankind also gradually lost the ability to follow cosmic law, to see the spiritual in the workings of the world. Not everyone lost this clairvoyance at the same time. Some lost it very quickly; for others it took a long time. In order to learn to live and be responsible only to himself and not to follow cosmic law, man had to separate from his cosmic homeland. In the China of 20,000 BC—while most of the people remained clairvoyant—some started to lose this ability. It was as though a spiritual blindness had settled on them. The old guidance had fallen away and now they were left to stand on their own. For those to whom this happened it was frightening and traumatic. They were terrified to persevere on their own without insight and guidance from the spiritual world. They searched for guidance to live an earthly life and asked others who were still clairvoyant to communicate to them what the spiritual world expected of them. As more and more people lost their clairvoyance there was sometimes only one clairvoyant left in a community who could relate what transpired in the spiritual world. These clairvoyant people were asked to give guidance and become leaders of the community. And when these leaders—who were among the last to have a connection to and perception of the spiritual world—died, the community searched until they found a new person who was clairvoyant. Then this person was designated to be their spiritual leader. Such a spiritual leader was called a priest. To this day we turn to priests and ministers, hoping they have a connection with the world of God, hoping they will give us meaningful answers.

Not only did the ancient community turn to the priest for help in spiritual matters, they also asked his advice in worldly affairs. And so, in time, the one who possessed insight in the laws of the cosmos was asked to be the secular leader too. In this way priest-kings and king-priests came into being. When a priest-king died the community searched for a new priest-king. Later, when even the priest-kings were no longer clairvoyant, it was proclaimed that the eldest son of the priest-king should be chosen to be the next priest-king. And so heredity became part of royal rule. While originally a king was selected by the people, his eldest son now became his successor by decree. For this reason the Pharaoh of ancient Egypt was both head of the church and head of the state. Even in our times this has its effects. In Great Britain the Queen serves as head of the Church of England. In Iran, as well, the Ayatollah led both the state and the church.

We must realize that being cut off from our spiritual origin was intentional and a necessary part of human evolution. If man was to become the entity that would bring freedom of choice into the cosmos, he had to learn to stand on his own, mindful of, but not bound by cosmic law. That is the reason why the ancient Chinese did not have religion. That is how religion came into being.

In reality, religion is the outer expression of our longing to re-align and reconnect with our origins in the spiritual world. The Old Testament shows us in eloquent word-pictures how, in the beginning of life on earth, man was not yet able to stand on his own and was strongly supported by the cosmos. This is beautifully illustrated in the stories of Moses. Frequent references are made to the relationship of God and Moses. In Exodus 33:11 it is related that "the Lord used to speak to Moses face to face, as a man speaks to his friend." In one of the most telling stories, God summons Moses to Mount Sinai. The mountain was ablaze and surrounded by smoke to hide the powerful presence of God from the people. Nonetheless these manifestations reflected the nearness of both God and the spiritual world and at the same time indicated the unmistakable separation of man from that world. It was in this setting that God delivered the Ten Commandments to Moses. These commandments were meant to serve as a guide for man's behavior on earth once his connection to the spiritual world was severed. This and many other Old Testament stories reveal how mankind was escorted and aided on his path to becoming responsible for himself on earth. In them we can observe that God and his messengers were directly involved in the lives of men, shepherding and tutoring mankind on its path of evolution. As time progressed and mankind matured, the involvement of these high spiritual beings in the affairs of mankind diminished. Mankind gradually adapted to life as an inhabitant of the earth rather than the cosmos and was ready to take responsibility for himself. A magnificent example of this can be found in one of the numerous stories about King Solomon. It is told that each of two women had given birth to a child; one baby died, but both women claimed the surviving child as her own. The women were brought before King Solomon who ordered the baby to be cut in two and half of the child given each women. One woman cried out and begged the King to let the baby live by giving it to the other woman. The second woman proclaimed it would be neither hers nor the first woman's, and declared that the child should be divided. King Solomon ruled that the first woman was the real mother and should have the baby. Through such stories about King Solomon, knowledge of his wisdom was made known to all. In these stories about King Solomon we encounter for the first time in the Old Testament the notion that decisions are no longer based upon revelations and guidance communicated by God or his messengers. The judgements are based solely on King Solomon's own earthly insights and wisdom.

In our time high spiritual beings no longer govern the course of human life. They observe our development from the spiritual world and note our progress. The dilemmas that confront us in life are now ours alone to solve. We must find our own way in life, and at the same time reestablish the connection with our spiritual origins. We no longer receive directives from the spiritual world telling us what is expected of us. We are completely free. The freedom of choice we have attained is ours to do with as we please. We can use this freedom to satisfy materialistic goals, or we can use it to advance the evolution of mankind, the earth, and the cosmos. Whichever path we choose, nothing and no one will interfere. The evolution of the earth and the cosmos is in our hands alone. In order to fulfill our task we need consciously to immerse ourselves in the purpose for earthly existence. We will never come to understand the meaning of life, nor will we make sense of the events of life, unless we discover for ourselves their underlying causes. Without an understanding of the causes, we will never be able to comprehend the effects.

VIII

PATHS OF INNER DEVELOPMENT

In the cosmos, life unfolds differently than it does on earth. On earth thinking, feeling, and willing are always intertwined. In everyday life there are no grounds for thinking unless our will or our feelings are also involved. In the spiritual world, however, thinking, feeling and willing are entirely separate functions. The spiritual world has three distinct realms: panorama, kamaloka and devachan. In each of these realms only one function has sovereignty—thinking, feeling, or willing. Thinking rules in panorama; we reflect without emotions and observe what occurred in our past life. In panorama we cannot act. Neither feeling nor will have sovereignty in panorama. Feeling reigns in kamaloka. We have emotions but cannot use our will. We have no possibility of avoiding the effects of our feelings; our will is nonexistent. Will prevails in devachan. Feeling and thinking in devachan are unlike they are on earth. It is through the exertion of our will that we are lead to our next incarnation.

On earth we have control over the activities of thinking, feeling and willing. During life on earth thinking, feeling and willing are permanently intertwined and each is kept in balance by the others. We could not read and understand these pages if this were not the case. Thinking and reading could not continue if our will were not urging us to persevere. And it is only because of our feelings that we are able to make sense of the words we read. Another example from everyday life can make this clear. Our stomach tells us it needs food; this hunger is a feeling. However, no action will take place unless we think about the consequence of this feeling of hunger. As a result of our thinking about our feeling of hunger, we decide that we need to eat. Still, no action occurs until we set our will in pursuit of something to eat. If we were to eliminate one of these three functions we would quickly find that the other two alone cannot support our existence on earth.

If we enter the spiritual world while we are alive on earth, thinking, feeling and willing instantly become independent of one another. If we have not consciously learned to master each individually, they overtake us and we are entirely at their mercy. When we enter the spiritual world in an unprepared way, the situation in which we put ourselves is extremely hazardous. The results of an unprepared entry into the spiritual world can be dangerous, even life threatening. We are confronted instantaneously with the inescapable reality of cosmic laws. Our will, feelings and thoughts immediately are subject to these laws and become independent of one another. Each goes its own unbridled way. We no longer have control over them. Anyone who has consumed too much alcohol is a clear-cut example of this. He exhibits loss of control over his will; his feelings overpower him; his thoughts are muddled. A bad trip on psychedelic drugs like LSD, cocaine or designer street drugs can provoke an even more violent confrontation with the spiritual world. A bad experience with these dangerous drugs gives the user an utterly frightening ordeal, much like going through kamaloka although still living on earth. The agony of watching someone go through such a drug experience is heartbreaking. A person under the influence of these drugs is confronted with the spiritual world, but his will is incapacitated. He endures the most terrifying emotions and is unable to stop them. He cannot flee and is scared to death. He is confronted with horrifying, devastating and overpowering feelings which he cannot restrain.

An entry into the spiritual world during life does not always have to be like this. There are safe and dependable practices we can learn to prepare ourselves properly to enter the spiritual world. For the time being let us call these training methods paths of inner development. The schooling we undergo on these paths is related to meditation. These paths are not short-cuts, like those induced by psychedelic drugs or alcohol, and they cannot be circumvented. If these paths are consciously and conscientiously pursued, they give the appropriate preparation to enter the spiritual world safely. It is imperative that we adequately prepare ourselves to face the inverted circumstances in the cosmos and learn to conduct ourselves in accordance with the laws which govern in the spiritual world. A path of inner development defines step by step what we must accomplish to consciously and competently enter the spiritual world.

We can characterize two established paths of inner development: Eastern, Oriental paths and a Western path. On Eastern paths we are guided by a master. His methods are proven and thousands of years old. The master knows all the dangers and risks on this path because he has traveled the same spiritual road and experienced the same threats. The master loves us. He knows that we feel insecure in life and bewildered by what we see around us. His peacefulness and serenity are consoling and reassuring. He prepares and trains us for every single step on this path and demands from us the strictest self-discipline. He meticulously monitors our progress and is attentive to every change we undergo. As long as we are guided by the master, not much can go wrong.

The master knows that the dangers on a path of spiritual development lie in the loss of control over our moral behavior, over the way we are able to think about what is right and wrong. When we commit ourselves to his path of inner development he will require us during our training to relinquish our ability to judge what is right and proper. We must surrender this willingly to our master. He will be our moral authority and we are secure as long as we rigorously follow his instructions. The master watches over us. With his guidance we learn how to meditate and how to lose interest in the content of our thoughts. He shows us how to detach ourselves from our thinking. There comes a point in our meditation exercises when he tells us that we have to become completely passive and allow ourselves to let go. All worldly images should leave us. Through his teaching we are lead to a stillness of thought called Satori. In Satori, the inner light, we find warmth and absolute peace. We unveil our inner being and become one with nature.

The master then leads us back to the beginning of our present incarnation. And if we allow ourselves to be guided without hesitation, we can be lead to former incarnations as well. He will help us to gain insight into occurrences in our former life and to find what influenced our decision to reincarnate. In this way he can lead us further and further back into our past. He will help us to peel away the karma we have built up during this incarnation and previous ones. The ultimate aim of Eastern paths is to return to the beginning of our first incarnation, to Paradise, to the primal beginning, to the state we had before the Fall of Man, to Nirvana. There we will encounter grace and bliss beyond time. These Eastern paths are many and varied; each has its own subtle nuances. But they all have in common a striving to reach back to Paradise, Nirvana, Satori, The Beginning. The training the Eastern master offers helps us to gain the inner strength required to reach this far back. Our whole life and entire existence will be directed towards this goal. We will be asked to renounce our body and abandon our urges and cravings. On the Eastern path only our soul-being counts. If we succeed, we will be liberated from earthly needs, as far as this is physically possible during life.

There are similarities between Eastern paths and the Western path. There are also great and significant differences. On the Western path we do not encounter a master. We travel this route on our own, in complete solitude. We are, at the same time, teacher and student. Although the steps have been mapped out for us, our success or failure is in our hands alone.

As on Eastern paths, the danger on the Western path lies in the loss of control over our moral conduct. On the Western path we do not have a master who evaluates our progress and the changes we go through. There is no subjective authority who binds us to his strict rules of moral discipline. We have to accomplish this ourselves. Only meticulous and scrupulous honesty towards our own moral stature will keep us properly on this path. We cannot allow ourselves to dissociate from the content of our thoughts or become completely passive. We must learn to determine for ourselves precisely what we are doing at any given moment. The training required by the Western path is arduous and it may take a long time to progress on this path. It demands that every step we take be retraceable, that every exercise we perform be repeatable. There are check-points, examinations which show us how far we have come, the dangers we might encounter. Each step on this path, rightly taken, will make us more inwardly secure and strong. When we have successfully traveled this road we will be able to enter the spiritual world with confidence. We will not be overcome by what we encounter there.

There are meditation exercises on the Western path that help us to train ourselves for a safe and conscious entry into the spiritual world. These exercises gradually lead us to the independent mastering of our thoughts, our feelings, and our will. There are numerous assignments, each designed to enhance one of these basic faculties; each is aimed at teaching us to acquire separate control of thinking, feeling or willing.

One such exercise out of a series of assignments to help us acquire absolutely clear thinking asks us to clear our mind of all ordinary thoughts and replace them by one single thought. This thought should be directed toward an uninteresting, not particularly important object. It is best to take a simple object, such as a fountain pen. The reason will soon become apparent. We should not put the object in front of us. We must concentrate on the thought of the chosen object for five minutes, without allowing other ideas to infiltrate our thoughts. It will not be long before we discover that our mind has wandered off and other thoughts have entered. We should not allow this to happen. But that is easier said than done.

Let us observe more closely our thoughts of the fountain pen. We imagine how a fountain pen looks, its size and color, how it was manufactured, the drawer in which we keep it in our desk, the store where we bought it. We can continue for a long time holding the idea of the fountain pen at the center of our thought. We try to sustain this exercise (this is an exercise, not a meditation), and remember a letter we wrote recently using this pen. We recall the pleasure we felt sharing some bit of good news with a faraway friend. We could hardly wait to affix a stamp to the envelope and drop it in the mail. While we daydream about this letter we realize suddenly that it was not our intention to contemplate our correspondence. Our original intent was to focus on a fountain pen. With this we come to realize how easily our thoughts wander off.

However keen we are to keep the thought of the fountain pen at the center of our attention, other thoughts always filter in. If we attempt to hold off infiltrating thoughts we discover how painstakingly difficult it is to concentrate on an insignificant object like a fountain pen, even for only five minutes. We can compare our thinking with a bowl filled with soup. Try to imagine using our fingers to keep the soup out of the middle of the bowl. The soup will always seep through our fingers, making it impossible for us to keep the center of the bowl free of soup. It is the same with our thinking. Only after weeks and months of practice will we be able to keep unrelated thoughts from filtering in. Had we chosen to think about a more complicated matter, like an airplane, a sunrise or the United States, we would not have detected so easily the difficulty in maintaining our train of thought.

Demanding as this first assignment may have seemed, the real training starts only after we have learned to concentrate for five minutes on the idea of the fountain pen without being lead astray. The next step is to imagine away our fountain pen. In the same way we have learned to push infiltrating thoughts out of our mind, we now must eliminate the thought of the fountain pen from our mind, without letting any other thought filter in. If we have been able to master pushing away all infiltrating thoughts, we might be proficient in this task. Our mind is then blank, a void with no thoughts. The greatest concentration and effort is required to achieve this void. It must be protected and preserved, kept empty of thoughts. When we have gained complete mastery of this part of the training, we will perceive that our ability to concentrate has increased. We will have acquired a new skill; we have become master of our thinking. Similar exercises exist to help become master of feeling and willing. They are well-defined and require the same self-discipline and practical approach to everyday situations that are found in the exercises for mastering thinking. These exercises seem to be straightforward, but adherence to the path defined by these practices necessitates personal perseverance and patience. Various books by Rudolf Steiner contain additional explanations of these meditative exercises.

There is a significant difference between the Eastern and the Western paths of inner development. Through both, the mind becomes void of thoughts. On the Eastern path, all thoughts dissipate through absolute passivity. On the Western path, it is not through passivity, but only through the most tenacious mental activity that we achieve command over our thoughts. On the Western path, the greatest concentration is required to master our thoughts and create this void.

In the exercise with the fountain pen and the thinking away of it, we actively create a void, an inner space. This inner space soon may begin to glow and radiate and become the center of an inner light. With this inner light, we find unequivocal peace. At first we need to undertake each step of the exercise anew to attain the stage of inner light. Later, through our will alone, we can create this inner light. We discover that we have become an instrument which will resonate to the whispers of the spiritual world. We have created and perfected this instrument through our own forces. There was no master asking us to submit ourselves to his discipline. We disciplined ourselves. Through these and the other exercises that comprise the Western path, we have become our own moral authority. On the Western path we learn how to become ruler of our thinking, as well our feeling and will, in order to comply with the laws which govern in the cosmos. When we have acquired these qualities we will have gained some of the qualities necessary to safely enter the spiritual world.

IX

CONSCIOUS ENTRANCE INTO THE SPIRITUAL WORLD

When we have progressed significantly on the Western path of inner development the spiritual world will test us to be certain we have the inner strength to withstand the confrontations we will encounter in the spiritual world. This examination is different from anything we ever experienced before, and we cannot fake its outcome. When we believe we are properly prepared and would like to enter the spiritual world, a cosmic being confronts us and blocks our access into the cosmos. The features of this being which obstructs our entry are horrifying and revolting. Only when we have achieved complete mastery over our thoughts, feelings and will, can we withstand its appearance. Even then, we still will want to flee. This cosmic being looks like our double. Its features are the manifestation of every evil deed we performed during all of our incarnations. We recognize this creature to be of our own creation. Each facet and every expression alludes to something that went wrong in this or a former life. No wonder that its unmasking is so shocking and revealing. At this point we are on the threshold of the spiritual world and already subject to cosmic law. We must withstand the truth emanating from the reality of this spiritual being. The effect of the meeting with this being is so intense that we need all our courage and presence of mind to withstand it. Only if we have achieved complete independent control of our feelings, will, and thoughts are we able to cope with this terrifying situation. If we have not built up enough inner strength to withstand this encounter, we are unable to face this being. At this moment we can still retreat and the confrontation will end. Even if this happens we will have made tremendous progress in our daily life. Although our retreat will have made it impossible for us to enter the spiritual world at this time, we will have strengthened our moral attitudes and moral discrimination as a result of our spiritual training. These reinforced moral characteristics will accompany us throughout the remainder of our life.

Every moral quality we acquire and every improvement of our soul we achieve during life will illuminate our continuing existence on earth. Furthermore it will be part of us after death. Moral characteristics originate in the cosmos and belong to cosmic law. If we learn to comprehend and master during our life on earth any law which reigns in the cosmic world, this law will be ours forever. The understanding of such a law will endure with us throughout this life, will continue to be part of us during our sojourn in the spiritual world, and will become an element of our character in our next incarnation. Nothing is ever lost in the universe. All our efforts—even a failed confrontation with this horrifying being—have meaning because moral virtues gained in one life become part of our character in our next life.

Let us return to our confrontation with this horrifying spiritual entity. Each facet of this being is the portrayal of an evil deed from our past; everything we see reminds us of a wicked deed. Every feature and detail is familiar to us. Only if we have mastery of our will, feelings, and thoughts can we withstand this confrontation at the threshold of the spiritual world. That is why this being is called the guardian of the threshold. This guardian does not grant us entrance into the spiritual world unless we can prove that we have achieved the courage and inner strength to withstand the confrontation with him. All our undertakings on our path of inner development have lead to this consequential point. What we have learned and what we have undergone find their culmination in this meeting with the guardian of the threshold. If we have achieved the complete authority over our thinking, feeling, and will imperative to prevail in this encounter, we also will have the strength required for what we will meet in the spiritual world.

When we have successfully withstood the confrontation with the guardian and are admitted into the spiritual world, we gain entry into a beautiful surrounding, constantly changing in shape, mood and appearance. This world is extremely pleasant, inspiring, and non-threatening. Now we must have at our command the other essential characteristic which reigns in the universe, morality.

Not only is it imperative that we master our individual thinking, feeling and willing, but we must also have attained a moral status which corresponds to cosmic law. If we have failed to achieve this moral status, our preparation and efforts to enter the spiritual world will have been in vain. Then our efforts will have been used to boost ourselves into the spiritual world without respect or awareness for its laws and values. Only when we have progressed and matured in a moral way will the guardian of the threshold grant us a merited entrance into the spiritual world.

When, as the result of a path of inner development, we consciously gain admittance to the spiritual world during life on earth, we view this world with earthly organs of perception. This is unlike our entry into the spiritual world after death, when we automatically must follow cosmic laws. When we penetrate the spiritual world during life, we cannot spontaneously follow these laws. Because we are earth beings, we must prepare and adapt ourselves before we enter. Because of our earthly perception, whatever we see in the spiritual world is distorted. We cannot trust what we see and experience. We think what we see is real and accurate, but it is not. With this we encounter an additional stumbling block. The images we encounter give the impression of reality, but these images are actually distortions of reality. We ourselves create these distortions. Let us use as an example a similar experience on earth. When we look into an aquarium from the top, we see the fish and plants at a specific location. If we look immediately into this aquarium from the side, the fish seem to be at a different spot then we saw from above. But viewed from the front they again seem to be at another place. Which of these views is the accurate one? Or think of what happens when we put a drinking straw in a glass of water. We know that the straw is straight and whole when we insert it. But from certain angles it looks as though it has been cut in two or bent. Pull the straw out and it is straight and whole again. In the spiritual world the images we perceive are distorted in much the same way that refraction altered our perception of the fish and the drinking straw. In the spiritual world, what we perceive is an inaccurate image of the reality. However, we are unaware that the picture is erroneous. We are unaware that the images are inexact and therefore we easily might describe our distorted impressions to others. Many psychics are not aware that the images they take in are distorted. They impart information about the spiritual world which is often deceptive. They relate half-truths, but do so in all innocence because they do not know better. Nevertheless, their indications often misrepresent the reality of the spiritual world. If we could correct the cause of the distortion, we could arrive at a more accurate description which might serve others. To see the reality we first must identify the distortions we added. We can learn to distinguish the distortion we are incorporating in the impression we see. We can become aware of these embellishments when we know who we are. In spiritual paths this is called *Know Thyself.*

This Know Thyself is a requirement on all spiritual paths. Only when we know ourselves, when we know the distortions we add to the images we perceive in the spiritual world, only then will we be able to transpose these images back to their true reality. Know Thyself is part of the Western spiritual training. We learn to know ourselves by investigating the meaning of a moral life and by living morally.

Through this Know Thyself we also will be able to inhibit the influence of the double, the being of evil that lives as a parasite in the cavities we created in our soul as a result of our past mistakes and evil deeds. We cannot separate ourselves from the double. It is a living entity which is attached to us for life. The double will do anything to weaken us both spiritually and physically so that we will be unable to resist its attacks from within. The double will use whatever means it can to undermine our resistance. It will attempt to sabotage our good intentions, to cripple our activities, to deteriorate our health, to reverse the improvements we already have made, to erode our morals, to break up our relationships, to impair our actions, to ruin our future. This is no doubt a terrifying picture, but we need only observe the world around us to see the reality and the accomplishments of the double.

We can defend ourselves against the double in only one way. That is to strengthen ourselves spiritually. Out of free choice we can decide to reduce or eliminate the cavities where he finds residence. The more moral, virtuous and honest our life, the more capable we are of reducing the cavities in which the double dwells. Virtues makes these cavities less inviting for the double. We do not have to wait until our next incarnation to constrict these cavities. We can already begin to live a moral life, here and now.

The encounter with the guardian of the threshold is one of the most significant dissimilarities between the Eastern and Western paths of inner development. On the Eastern path we do not meet the guardian of the threshold. Eastern paths allow us to go backwards on the wheel of incarnation until it theoretically would be possible to reach Nirvana. On the Eastern path of spiritual training we go back on the wheel of incarnation, stripping off accumulated karma and breaking down the double. We return to Paradise or Nirvana, to the time we did not yet have a double, to the time when we did not yet have karma.

The Western path has an entirely different objective. On the Western path we must meet the guardian of the threshold. We perform more deeds, take on more tasks and harvest more karma. On the Western path we go onward in our successive incarnations and proceed toward fulfilling the task of mankind. On the Eastern path we return on the wheel of incarnation and strip off karma. We redeem ourselves, but not mankind.

Why is it imperative that we follow this laborious Western path when there are proven Eastern ways that have been around for thousands of years? Since these ancient Eastern paths were introduced, mankind has gone through an immense development. Man of today is not the same as he was 5,000 years ago. These ancient teachings, which were pertinent and valid when mankind was still partly clairvoyant, do not accomplish the same spiritual objective for modern man. Why is it that the path to reach the spiritual world has changed so completely? Why is the Eastern path that had such immeasurable significance in times past no longer valid today? What transpired for such a turnabout to take place, and why did the Western path emerge?

The ancient Eastern paths directed us to the spiritual world by peeling off accumulated karma, by leading us back on the wheel of incarnations. In those times it was the only accurate and effective access to the spiritual world; other approaches did not exist. Then, two thousand years ago an unprecedented event took place. A God-being, Christ, came to the earth and merged its destiny with the destiny of mankind in order to alter the future completely. Before Christ came to the earth—after clairvoyance had begun to fade—the only way to connect with the cosmos had been the Eastern initiation paths. On these ancient paths of initiation only a few carefully chosen and prepared individuals were allowed to achieve the level of wisdom needed to gain conscious access to the spiritual world. With the coming of Christ an unprecedented and unique access was revealed. This new Christian path not only established unique, previously unknown conditions for gaining entrance to the spiritual world, it also entirely changed the direction in which the evolution of mankind was headed. Spiritual advancement was no longer the privilege of those chosen individuals who followed the ancient Eastern initiation paths. From the moment Christ united his destiny with the earthly life of mankind, the conscious road to the spiritual world was opened to every individual. It became possible for every human being on his own—without the intercession of church or priest—to participate in the progress of the whole of mankind. Furthermore, the one who pursues the Western Christian path of initiation is not only serving his own development, but in addition works on the further advancement of the cosmos. As we have seen from the outset, this is the mission for mankind. For mankind Christ became the Lord of Karma. The evolution of mankind and the universe has reached new directions as the result of the association of Christ with the future of mankind.

We must realize that karma is not a set number of actions we must perform during life. Nor is it a drama with the lines already written. Karma expands, just as our moral horizon can expand. Let us use a metaphor. Imagine we are crossing a barren desert. On the horizon we see a palm tree. We go toward the horizon and reach the palm tree. Although we have reached the tree, the horizon has moved. Karma proceeds in much the same way. There is more karma to compensate for than can be accomplished in one lifetime. Karma represents the hindrances we have to overcome in this life and in the future.

Although we can not always substitute the one for the other, karma, the double and the guardian of the threshold are three expressions for the same challenge. We are afraid to talk about the double and the guardian of the threshold, but so casually exclaim: "Oh, but that's your karma." Nonetheless, they represent one and the same. Karma is the opportunity and challenge to redeem the wrongful deeds from our past. Our character is also an expression of our karma. By improving our character and eliminating our bad habits we work on ourselves, on our karma, and our future incarnations.

X

MORALITY, LOVE, AND SEXUAL DESIRE

On our path of inner development we meet the guardian of the threshold. If we are admitted to the spiritual world we perceive images there that need to be translated into their true reality. We can do this only if we are living a moral life. The training which leads to the meeting with the guardian of the threshold also teaches us how to be a moral person by granting the opportunity to judge for ourselves the level of morality we have been able to achieve during our earth incarnation.

The moral characteristics and virtues we acquire during life on earth remain with us after death. They are imprinted on our soul and during devachan become part of the kernel of our spirit. When we return in our next incarnation, these virtues will be elements of our new character. The moral characteristics acquired in a former incarnation become an intrinsic part of our ego. These moral qualities inspire us on our individual evolutionary path; they make us more perfect and enable us to fulfill the task for which we came to earth.

The moral progress of every individual is therefore his responsibility alone. Some people are very swift in their moral development. Others are closed-minded and feel no need to go any further. They contend that life is excellent just the way it is. "Why should I be moral?" "If I can't make a buck with it, what good is it?" "I want to live in the fast lane." "My life is too busy to think about morality." "I do the best I can under the circumstances." "I'm no philosopher, so don't expect me to think about morality." We often hear such remarks from people around us. There seems to be no point in telling them that there is more to life than material wealth or just getting by. Any and all arguments only fall on deaf ears.

Morality is not the product of the imagination of philosophers or theologians. Morality is objective substance which originates in the cosmos. Earthly moral qualities actually are invisible spiritual characteristics. If we behave in an increasingly moral way during life, these hard won earthly moral qualities will make it possible for us to absorb additional cosmic moral substance when we return to the spiritual world after death. Ultimately we will bring this moral substance back into a new incarnation as an integral part of our character. As a result, in our new life we will be a nobler human being.

Whatever cosmic morality and cosmic truth we attain by our deeds and put to use during life on earth will be ours forever. They will become part of our character in our next incarnation in what we call our conscience, our so-called good conscience. Every rung we ascend on the ladder of moral life is an endowment for our personality in subsequent incarnations. If we have attained moral qualities during life, these virtuous features will stay with us when we return to the cosmos at death. During the period between death and rebirth, cosmic moral principles surround us, but at birth we lose all conscious knowledge of spiritual truths. During our earthly life we must endeavor to be ethical and acquire moral principles consciously. Every improvement of this kind we make throughout the course of our whole life has meaning and is important. This is how we are able to cultivate ourselves and become better equipped for our task as human beings.

Each of us must attain on our own an understanding of cosmic truth and cosmic moral principles. This understanding cannot be forced upon us; it is part of the progress we make on our individual path of inner development which leads to freedom of choice. We assume our new incarnation with the moral standing we attained in our previous incarnation. This is true for all the cosmic wisdom we achieve. In the beginning we asked: "Is life significant?" Well, the results of our progress provide an answer.

Through our investigations we are gradually coming to recognize that noble human qualities like morality originate in the cosmos. We will find that this is particularly true of the most ennobling of human cosmic qualities—love. Love originates in the cosmos. When we looked at love, we concluded that the foundation of human love lies in the remembrance of shared experiences with other beings with whom we were united in the spiritual world. Until now we only discussed the love we feel for individuals, like family members, our children, our friends. However, the love that can lead to intimacy between a man and a woman is at once one of the most intriguing subjects and one of the most enigmatic. Again, the seed for such intimate relationships can be discovered and better appreciated when we bring to mind our spiritual origins.

As we have said, during our sojourn in the spiritual world we encounter one another differently than we do on earth. In the cosmos we communicate by trying to mirror the spiritual configuration of the soul; we approach. We try to mimic the spiritual presence of the other soul. If our encounter is successful we behold the essence of that soul; we merge with and penetrate one another. We respond to the feelings, impressions, emotions, sympathies, and affections of the other. However, even during these moments of spiritual intimacy we retain our own individuality; gender does not exist in the cosmos.

These facts lead us to some of the most basic questions we can ask about loving and intimate relationships on earth—why are we born female or male and why are we attracted to the opposite gender? We can identify some representative female characteristics. Generally speaking a woman's figure is more rounded and she has softer skin. She is more sensitive and has an affinity to care for others. A woman is perceptive and intuitive, gentler, more compassionate and accommodating. Appreciation of female characteristics vary with time. Modern society denies many of these perceptions of womanhood and femininity; but, as a rule, these characteristics certainly cannot be attributed to the male gender. If we consider some typical male traits, we find that a man's features are more angular and he is rougher in his stance. A man is commanding, aggressive in his dealings with others, and his attention is directed more to the outside world. Whatever picture we paint of the male, one thing is absolutely certain—he differs from a female and not only in his genitals. Of course there are exceptions to every generality. But, putting all feminism aside, a woman is different from a man and a man is different from a woman.

It is common knowledge that men need women and women need men, even if it is only for procreation. We all know there is more to our desire than physical attraction and the continuation of the species. In ordinary situations a man and a woman feel fulfilled when they are together. In almost every human being there is a yearning for the opposite gender. Even at an early age our fondness and desire for the other sex is present and usually stays with us until death. The loving tenderness with which some older couples treat one another is a touching example.

Our longing for the other gender lies deep in us and this has an immense influence on society as a whole. Sexual longing is used and quite often misused in many ways. Most of the programming on network TV would disappear if the attraction for the other sex was eliminated from the story lines. Advertisements and commercials emphasize sexuality in order to sell every conceivable product. In addition we are continually bombarded with book covers and a multitude of publications that suggest sex appeal is necessary for success in life.

Although it is our nature to be attracted to the other sex, we cannot become the other gender. When we die we still have this longing for the opposite sex. However, as we have said, gender does not exist in the cosmos. Our curiosity for what made the other tick, as well as for what the other sex might have had that we ourselves did not, results in an inclination to become the other gender in our next incarnation. As a consequence we change gender the next time we assemble our karma and incarnate. As a rule we may say, if one incarnation is female, the next one will be male.

Once in a conversation with a successful businessman we came to speak about how gender alternates in subsequent incarnations. He had been very open-minded and willing to accept the logic in our explanations of the realities of life. However when he found out about the alternation of gender, he exploded. His anger actually was ludicrous. His whole life had been based on the idea that as a male he was better than any female. This revelation completely pulled the rug out from under him. It was too much for him to imagine that his next life might be spent as a woman. He had degraded, denounced and criticized females his whole life and had associated them with everything he disliked. He had ridiculed women wherever and whenever he could, only to discover that in his next life he most probably would be a female. Here again we see a manifestation of the law of karma. In kamaloka our businessman will find out for himself that everything rebounds. When he is confronted with this fact in kamaloka, it already will be too late for him. He cannot evade the humiliation that results from the deeds he performed.

When we return to earth in a new incarnation—to fulfill a next life on earth—we clothe our ego in a physical body. This physical body enables our ego to perform deeds during life on earth. The ego, which is an entirely spiritual entity, cannot experience directly anything earthly. During life on earth, the soul must translate for the ego what we experience outwardly. The ego needs the soul to interpret for the ego what the soul experiences in the outer world. The ego also needs the soul to express what resounds in the ego itself. However, the soul has difficulty expressing its experiences in mere words. For example, try to convey in words the feeling of homesickness, the rage of anger or the glow of love. In our soul, we know exactly what these emotions are, but words fail us when we want them to convey the depth of our feelings. The moment we attempt to express the emotional fervor in our soul, difficulties instantly arise. If we try to circumvent the problem, we find that even alternate approaches lead no further. Having a feeling and verbalizing a feeling are two very different ventures.

Keeping in mind this inability of words to express our feelings adequately, let us return to the question of an intimate relationship between a man and a woman. From what we have already said, we know that the circumstances of a meeting are the result of shared karma. The ways we meet one another on earth are as many and varied as the stars in the night sky. However, what makes this encounter stand out from the rest is that we are drawn to one another by an almost tangible and, at the same time, inexplicable bond. Although in this incarnation the physical appearance of the other being is new to us, we recognize again his or her familiar spiritual essence. In the most subtle ways, the reality of our recognition is made known to us—an exchange of glances, a gesture seen out of the corner of an eye, a fleeting memory of a shared experience that could not have happened in this life, even the unexplainable memory of a familiar scent. We feel an undeniably warm and loving connection and an awareness that this encounter is remarkable and rare. The familiarity hardly feels of this world. There is a mutual closeness and an affinity that allows us to trust one another with the most profound secrets of our hearts. Nothing stops us from opening up completely to one another. Companionship and friendship grow into respect and devotion. Our friend is in harmony with our tender feelings. This affinity transforms our fondness for one another into feelings of adoration, love, and physical desire. Our emotions, our feelings of tenderness, and the intimacy of the situation lead to a yearning for the fulfillment of our love. The attraction grows more intense with each encounter. A caress, an embrace and a kiss lead inevitably to passion, and we make love. Towering desire and our longing for intimacy bring us to heavenly heights. Our mounting passions culminate in a divine climax and for a moment we are gone from this world.

In reality that is precisely what happens. A sexual climax takes us out of ourselves, out of this world, and for a brief moment returns us to the spiritual world. During a sexual climax we leave our physical body and experience once again the spiritual union we attained in the cosmos. We lose awareness of what is happening on the physical plane and for a glorious moment we are purely spiritual. We are united just as we were in the spiritual world. We feel what our lover feels. Since we are inhabitants of the earth, we cannot dwell indefinitely in this highly elevated, orgasmic state. We must return to our earthly environment. However, we carry the memory of this spiritual paradise with us, and therefore we always long to recapture this intimate union.

This is the cause and the reality of our sexual desire. Our sexual desire is proof and confirmation of our spiritual origin. Our physical attraction and sexual desire are based on our yearning to return to the celestial interpenetration we achieved while we were in the spiritual world. Our sexual longing actually has the most esoteric origin. Who would have ever dared to imagine that our so-called lower lusts illustrate the fact that we are spiritual beings? Yet if we re-examine the circumstances of ordinary life from this unusual perspective, time after time we are given proof that our true heritage is spiritual, not of this world.

How did we lose sight of this fact? What distorts and perverts the purity of our yearning to reunite with the one we revered in the spiritual world? Lucifer and Ahriman. As we said earlier, Lucifer and Ahriman want to confuse us about their intentions toward us. They combine their efforts and distract us with half-truths so that we never can determine the source of our problems.

The difficulties we encounter in intimate relationships are an obvious example of the influence of Ahriman in our lives. To Ahriman the bliss of our sexual union is clear; he knows that the ego within our physical body longs to rediscover and recognize on earth that special being we revered in the spiritual world. He is aware that when we make love with the one we were united with in the spiritual world, we will be reminded of our spiritual intimacy and through this will come to remember our spiritual origin. That would be altogether contrary to his goals. So he diverts our attention from the spiritual reality of human relationships and focuses it instead on our physical desire. Ahriman tells us: "You are aroused and excited. Make love. Have a good time. Surely, by making love, you will see that your partner is meant to be someone special in your life. In this warm and sensuous state, you'll feel as though you're in heaven. If you were delighted by the outcome of this encounter, try it again. And you do not have to limit your pleasure by making love with just this person. The world is full of attractive people. Make love with anyone you want and you can create that glowing feeling of heavenly bliss both of you long for."

While Ahriman tells us this, he knows that this is not the way loving and intimate relationships were meant to work. Ahriman knows full well that the more we make love with countless, different partners, the more disturbed we will be when things do not work out as we hope. He is aware that the recollection of the intimacy we shared with a loved one in the spiritual world is the reason for our feelings of tenderness and the glow of love. He also knows that if we make love with someone we never had a relationship with in the spiritual world, the feeling of recognition and the glow of love can never be achieved. Through the subtlety of his deceit Ahriman hopes we will become so entangled in the emotional discomfort and difficulties of our relationships that we will never recognize the reasons for our failures. He will then have succeeded in leading us astray.

XI

CONSEQUENCES OF SUICIDE

As individuals living on earth, our task is to achieve freedom of choice in order to create independence from cosmic law. Of course, we need the experience and wisdom of others to guide and teach us. Through encounters with others our interests and enthusiasm are fired up. An honest conversation can be heartwarming and uplifting. As a result of such interactions, we can see unexpected new ways, discover unexplored frontiers and often find the courage to forge ahead. On our own we would not have discovered such possibilities so easily. The support of others can help us in learning to stand on our own, but we should not rely on others to make decisions for us. In this respect, our educational system does not always prepare us to assume the responsibility of standing on our own. Some established, accepted educational methods and practices even hamper learning and development. Children are trained to depend on calculators, computers and other hardware to perform tasks which otherwise would require more time or could not have been accomplished alone. The primary danger of this new equipment is that it subtly teaches us to rely only on new and intriguing technology for answers. We must be attentive to the fact that the potential also exists for this technology to hamper our ability to complete tasks on our own.

When we encourage young children to spend their time mastering the computer at the expense of traditional childhood activities, their ability to understand life creatively can be thwarted. Look carefully at those children, who at the age of five were delighted to learn about computers and to play computer games. They seemed to thrive in the midst of the technology with which they were raised. Caught up in the enthusiasm of doing the right thing, their parents spent a fortune and were confident they were helping their children to develop the talents that would give them an edge in their adult lives. These children got the message that this is the way to succeed in life. However, as these children grew up it became clear that something was absent from their lives; they were unable to cope with seemingly common situations. They lacked the social skill of conversation, the ability to communicate feelings, and share heartwarming human encounters. They did not learn to meet others with tenderness or compassion. Instead their efforts were spent mastering sophisticated, electronic tools. They developed only the minimum social skills required to cope with life.

When these children become young adults, they frequently feel they cannot make human connections and are often overcome by despair. They do not know how to articulate their feelings. Their responses to human situations are clumsy. Like all of us, these adolescents need kindness and sympathy. Yet, when they receive warmth and affection they are unable to manage their emotions. These teen-agers know there is supposed to be more to life, but their education and upbringing did not give them the chance to develop a healthy feeling life. They never found within themselves the capacity to communicate openly and sympathetically with others. These lonesome teens are afraid to be on their own; they always look for superficial distractions. When we meet them we sense their alienation from life. They immerse themselves in electronic gadgets and seem to be fascinated, even spellbound, by material possessions. In reality, they are afraid to confess their loneliness. They dare not admit to anyone that they feel alienated from life. Such an admission would mean they fall short of their parents expectations and are failing in life. If no one were to step in to provide help, these teenagers could fall even more deeply into despair. They might commit acts the adult world would neither fathom nor comprehend. Tragically, their emotional distress can lead even to suicide. The key to solving the tragedy of teenage suicide will be found only when parents and educators actively pursue life with the knowledge that we all are incarnate spiritual beings. They must awaken to the fact that the spiritual nature of the children in their care needs to be nurtured and carefully safeguarded if it is to lead these children to a moral and healthy adult life. The lack of such knowledge has far-reaching consequences on earth as well as in the spiritual world.

Let us consider what happens to someone who has taken his own life. From our earlier discussions of death we can conclude that the after-life experience of someone who committed suicide will not be pleasant. If we have the courage to think it through, we will uncover for ourselves some of the spiritual repercussions of this tragic deed. When someone commits suicide, he abandons life and returns to the spiritual world. However, he soon finds that his death is hardly the relief from the anguish of life he had imagined it would be. Kamaloka does not begin immediately after death for someone who has taken his own life. He becomes trapped between panorama and kamaloka, and remains paralyzed there until the moment his natural death—the moment that was predetermined when the karma for this life was planned—would have taken place. He is stunned and bewildered remembering the aspirations he had for his impending life before it even began. He painfully becomes aware that he has failed. He recognizes that he did not face the tasks or fulfill the goals he had set for himself. Instead, he chose to forsake the challenges of life. Objectively, but in no way dispassionately, he perceives the agonizing and far-reaching results of the destruction of his own life. And while realizing this, he faces the fact that it is too late to change the past. Aghast and horrified he suffers this humiliation for what would have been the remainder of his predetermined earth-life. He finds himself transfixed, terrified and benumbed. For the duration of all those years until the moment his natural death should have taken place, he must endure the consequences of his last decision—that life was not livable. He, who sought to escape the burdens of earthly life, is now bound to this last earthly decision. He desperately wants to begin kamaloka, to clean up the mess he made of his life and to burn off his mistakes. But his decision is irreparable. He is trapped in a blind alley of his own making until the moment of his natural death. Stranded on the threshold of kamaloka, he is in utter despair, knowing that he failed to accomplish the tasks he had planned to fulfill on earth. He is mortified by the shame and degradation that are the unavoidable spiritual results of suicide. He feels the full impact of the humiliation to which he has condemned himself.

When he finally enters kamaloka at the predetermined time of his natural death, he is overcome by the guilt of having failed himself as well as his task for mankind. These feelings of guilt will persist as long as he remains in the spiritual world. And in his new incarnation these same feelings will reemerge in an extremely insecure character. In everything he undertakes, he will be afraid to fail. These are the people we meet who always fall short of their own and other people's expectations. We should be especially kind and compassionate to them. In their new incarnation they must learn not to withdraw from life; they must find the courage to conquer the obstacles of life. But through suicide, they added to their path the burden of continually feeling inferior and inadequate.

This is a frightening picture; but it is imperative to realize that suicide is not an easy way out or a release from the burdens of life. Here again we catch a glimpse of the significant influence of the law of karma in our daily life. Every action we perform during earthly life has its consequence, during this life as well as in a subsequent incarnation. That is the law of karma.

XII

HOW THE DOUBLE WORKS

We are not aware of the presence of the double continuously; but, once in a while, we are so obviously shaken by something that happens, that we are rudely awakened to its active role in our life. The double lives in the cavities in our soul we are unable to reach, the cavities created as a result of our mistakes in former lives. It is made up of ahrimanic entities that live in us as spiritual parasites, and which take great delight in disrupting our lives. Certain kinds of arguments are typical of the way the double does his work. A discussion we once had with our spouse or friend may have started out as a conversation about something utterly trivial and innocent. All of a sudden, the conversation began to deviate from it's original course. Before we knew it, our cordial conversation had deteriorated into something ugly and mean. We lost control and things were said which ordinarily would never come to mind, things we did not mean and which we now honestly regret. We never planned for our conversation to become a disagreement, but all of a sudden, our good intentions had vanished into thin air. Turmoil ensued. Afterwards, we might have had the greatest difficulty remembering the particulars of what actually occurred. Enormous energy and effort were required to clean up the mess, to salve hurt feelings and mend the relationship. How could this have happened so quickly, so unexpectedly?

Everyone has experienced similar situations. We know first hand how they can abruptly jeopardize a relationship. What actually happened? Our double and the double of our spouse or friend waited to catch us off guard in a situation just like this. In this case, our doubles found us in a weak moment—perhaps our thoughts were preoccupied with something else—and they leapt at this opportunity. The argument occurred, the words came from our mouths; but, in fact our doubles were speaking through us. The doubles took over, unexpectedly. Our double put these hurtful words in our mouth and it did so because we did not have enough inner strength and stability to withstand its influence. This is only one example of a situation where the double takes over. There are countless more.

We also can experience the power of the double through the misuse of alcohol. Originally alcohol was used in connection with religious practices. The remnants of this are visible in the symbolic use of wine in the celebration of religious rituals in many faiths. Why is this? The use of wine for such purposes dates to the founding of religion itself, to the time of the first priest-kings and king-priests. As one of the last clairvoyant members of the community, it fell to them to be both its spiritual and secular leader. Through his remaining clairvoyant connection with the spiritual world and cosmic law, the priest knew that the task of achieving freedom of choice required mankind to separate itself completely from the spiritual world. In order to perform his task the priest realized that he, too, had to be independent of cosmic law to a certain degree. Wine and alcohol provided the release from cosmic law that these priests needed to serve the needs of their earthly communities. The sacramental use of wine made it possible for the priest to feel more fully incarnate by temporarily severing his ties with the spiritual world.

For humanity much has changed since those ancient times. Mankind has traveled a long evolutionary path. Much of what was required spiritually in the past is no longer valid today. We know all too well the effects of alcohol on the human being. Alcohol clouds our thinking and dims awareness of our individuality. When this happens, we too are cut off from the spiritual world. Alcohol makes us forget anything spiritual, just as it did in the past for the priests. In our time—because we are on the threshold of regaining clairvoyance—we need to connect with, rather than disengage ourselves from the spiritual world. Alcohol counteracts the progress we may have already made and obstructs the continuing development on our evolutionary path.

The effects of alcohol on the human physical and spiritual

bodies are known to the double. Alcohol enlarges the cavities where these ahrimanic entities reside in our soul. These same ahrimanic entities gloat with joy when we consume alcohol, because it allows them more leeway in which to exert their influence over us. Alcohol weakens us, upsetting the delicate balance of power between our ego and the double. Alcohol gives the ahrimanic entities the space they want to become stronger, to be more powerful and aggressive. The relationship that normally exists between our ego and our double is brought out of equilibrium through the use of alcohol. When we consume alcohol we hand these ahrimanic entities the opportunity to be more vigorous in their attacks on us. In our weakened condition the influence of the double grows ever more effective. In turn, our vulnerability to these ahrimanic beings increases. As a result, more often than we would care to admit, we come out the loser.

Ahriman is exceedingly pleased when we consume alcohol, because his foremost goal—to make us forget our spiritual origin—is greatly served by this practice. Without protest or objection from us—indeed, usually with our own hearty compliance—Ahriman pours down our throats the elixir that makes us forget our cosmic origins. Alcohol is Ahriman's silent, but very effective partner.

An entirely different result of the double's hold on our life can be discovered if we turn our attention to geography and the place where we reside. It is well known that the earth has magnetic North and South poles. Between them run magnetic lines of force which can be followed with a magnetic compass. The intensity of these magnetic forces and the magnetic lines of force vary in strength in different locations of the earth. These variations in strength of the magnetic forces are known to be related to the size and position of nearby mountain ranges. A mountain range which lies at right angles to these magnetic forces diminishes them, while a mountain range that runs parallel to the magnetic lines of force intensifies and increases them.

A simple experiment can better demonstrate this fact. We will need a small magnet, some iron filings, a piece of cardboard, and some ordinary iron nails of different sizes. If we spread the iron filings on the cardboard we will see that they distribute randomly over it. When we place the magnet under the cardboard the iron filings arrange themselves in a particular pattern. If we tap lightly on the cardboard, the iron filings form strands along invisible lines. These lines are the lines of force of the magnet. The pattern of these lines is specific to this particular magnet. Exactly the same pattern will appear every time we position the magnet at the same spot and the same distance under the cardboard. If we now place a nail among the iron filings on the cardboard, we will notice that the filings arrange themselves along the length of the nail. The lines of force converge around the nail. The sturdier the nail, the more tightly the lines of force converge along it.

Similar phenomena can be found on earth. The magnetic lines of force of the earth run from the North Pole to the South Pole. Mountain ranges that run from east to west, like the Alps in Europe and the Himalayas in Asia weaken the strength of the nearby magnetic lines of force. The Rocky Mountains and the Andes in the Americas run north and south and intensify the strength of the magnetic lines of force in proximity to them. Not only do these mountain ranges alter the strength of these magnetic forces, they also shift the direction slightly, not unlike the effect we observed with the magnet, the iron-filings and the nail.

Magnetic forces also alter the size of the soul cavities in which the ahrimanic entities reside in us. The soul cavities expand when the influence of the magnetic forces becomes stronger. The size of the cavities increases as a result of the intensification of the magnetic forces, just as they do in the case of the use of alcohol. When the cavities become enlarged, we need more inner strength and power to keep the double at bay. As was indicated earlier, the double—comprised of these ahrimanic entities—must be held in balance by our ego. We need to have authority over our double, or without question we will become its puppet.

Businessmen who travel frequently notice that their reactions to life and work situations are different in various parts of the world. They are aware that life on the West Coast is more frenzied, frenetic and frantic. When they travel to the West they experience an increased dominance of the double. Even travellers from the East Coast who are unaware of the existence of the double are well aware of a change in the way they react to ordinary situations on the West Coast. If they are wise they realize that during their stay in the West they must be more alert when making arrangements or decisions. If they are not keenly attentive they may succumb to the entrapment of the double. Important decisions which would have taken days of deliberation at home are made within hours. The usual healthy judgment that typically would go into the conclusions they draw is lacking. In the location where they ordinarily reside it is unlikely they would have made the same decision. These reactions have many names—for some this is called California Fever; others call it Granola Syndrome.

Just the opposite happens when someone who lives in the West travels on the East Coast. He is so accustomed to the strong presence of the double in the West that when he travels East he does not trust his own judgement. For someone whose home is on the West Coast, life seems to flow too smoothly, too easily in the East. The clearest examples of this can be observed in people who travel from the West Coast to Europe or Asia. For them, the soul cavities in which the double resides become smaller. Less inner force is needed to withstand the influence of the double. Life seems to become inexplicably effortless. We sometimes hear about couples who live in the West that traveled on the East Coast for an extended period. Their trip East was peaceful, harmonious and pleasant. When they returned home, they ran into great personal difficulties for no apparent reason. The harmony which united them during their travels was shattered. In reality, upon returning to the West, the doubles of each regained their ordinary strength and the vigor with which these doubles reemerged took the couple by surprise. The double of each was able to have a field day with their host and the chaos it could create in the couple's lives. All of these difficulties were affected by the magnetic forces of the earth.

Computer terminals, TV, and fluorescent lighting likewise have an equivalent effect on our ability to withstand the double. These electrical and electronic devices emit electromagnetic energies which are similar to, but much more powerful and concentrated than the earth's magnetic forces. When we are placed in the focus of these electromagnetic fields and bombarded by their electromagnetic forces, the effect these forces can have on us may be overpowering. The strength of these electromagnetic forces is many times more intense than the magnetic force of the earth. The double is invigorated by these electromagnetic forces. We can imagine the effect these much stronger electromagnetic forces might have, if we recall the effect California Fever has on people. Nonetheless, our contact with this technology does not have to have devastating results. Our first reaction to this situation might have been: "If this electronic equipment has such a subtle and devastating effect on us, why don't we simply get rid of all of it?" Such a solution may sound logical, but we are living in an age where this equipment is part and parcel of everyday life. We cannot return to the conditions of prehistoric civilization; technology belongs to modern society and to our lives. Modern conveniences have been put on our path and we must face the challenges they present. Instead of turning our back on them or giving in to them completely, we should strengthen our resistance to their harmful influence. There are Western meditative techniques to counter the increased influence of the double. We can learn them when we follow the Western path of inner development.

XIII

Overcoming Fear

If we acknowledge the presence of the double in our lives, certain questions may arise: "Before birth while we were in the spiritual world we were able to envision everything that would take place in our next life. Why then would we have decided to be born in the United States and spend our lives here? Couldn't we have found some other place to live?" As we planned our next life we certainly could have chosen a different place to be born and to live. While we were in the spiritual world we had the chance to arrange the circumstances and situations we would have to face in life in order to fulfill our karma. We consciously chose to be born in the United States, knowing the challenges we would meet here at the end of the twentieth century. We continually are told that the air we breathe and the water we drink are polluted, the food we eat is contaminated, the streets of our cities unsafe. Yet, before we were born we chose to have a life here, because we knew we needed the opposition that life in this country, at this time would provide, and that we would be able to manage these challenges. We wanted these challenges because we knew they would give us opportunities to become mentally, physically and spiritually stronger. We wanted to be born and to live in the United States because we knew we would come out stronger for having met these challenges. Before birth we knew we would have the courage as well as the inner strength not to succumb to these stumbling blocks. When we were born we made the commitment to conquer these obstacles. In this way we could progress on our individual path as well as serve the evolution of mankind. This is why we chose to be born in the United States in an era, in a world teeming with confusion.

It is easy to see why so many people feel alone, confused and alienated. The demands on us are enormous. In the world today there seem to be no genuine ethical values. Reliable guidance is nearly impossible to find. The role models we are provided profess beliefs we find inappropriate and their values seem obsolete. We feel we have no choice but to reject them. Even if we do not experience this alienation ourselves, we see it in the relationships of our friends and colleagues. Divorce is more common than living together harmoniously for thirty, forty, and fifty years. And when we look at the couples who are still married, we wonder if they are happy that way or if they are merely clinging to each other out of fear or obligation. Increasingly, we find this an unacceptable way to live. Where can we find the right role models now that they seem no longer to exist? And how are we to raise our children when we ourselves have not inherited true and lasting values? There are no longer set rules for how to live. Definite standards no longer exist. Many men and women view success and prestige exclusively in terms of money and materialistic rewards. Do honesty and reliability still count? Not if we examine the evidence presented in the media. Lying and getting away with it seem more profitable than honesty. It is difficult to have faith in those in authority or the government. No one admits responsibility anymore. Is there anyone in whom we can still place our confidence? How can we be expected to grow up responsibly—to raise children who will lead civilization into the 21st century—when virtually all the examples we are presented with are barely disguised incidents of corruption and dishonesty? Dumps are filled with toxic waste which harms and burdens us, leaving generations to come with the clean-up. Our predecessors left behind an unfathomable obligation in the form of the national deficit, pollution, poverty, and God only knows what else. Are these the models that we want to shepherd and guide the next generation? Unless we now create our own virtues, our children too will inherit the mistakes and problems of the past.

As we consider these occurrences in our lives we can begin to understand how fear has become one of the most pressing issues of our time. Fear of nuclear war, fear of toxic pollution, fear of deadly illness, fear of physical assault. The future looks thoroughly depressing. And that is exactly what Ahriman wants us to think. If we allow these situations to get the best of us, if we lose heart and panic, we soon find that we are unable to defend ourselves. If we surrender to fear we fall prey to Ahriman and give him an easy victory over us. Ahriman will go to any extreme to achieve his goal of strangling us with fear. Each time we succumb, every time we allow Ahriman to succeed there is one less human being opposing his evil influence. We must therefore examine fear and what we can do in our daily lives to overcome it. Even though we can only scratch the surface here, an examination of fear still can provide us food for thought and a first step towards loosening the grip Ahriman and fear have on all of us.

The causes of fear are different for each of us, even though our responses to it are strikingly similar. When we become frightened, we panic and lose control. Instead of acting, we react. As a result, we may end up in a more upsetting situation than the one which first caused us to panic. In addition, we might become so paralyzed that we dare not move at all. Unfortunately, as we have already discussed, in our time there are many frightening situations that lead to this kind of paralysis. We only need to think about elderly people who are afraid to open the front door or to take the risk of shopping on their own. Many people tremble with fear when their car breaks down in an unfamiliar neighborhood or on a desolate road. The ruinous effects of drugs on our society leaves us feeling threatened and helpless. This is exactly how Ahriman and Lucifer try to undermine us. They want us to feel so incompetent and unprotected, intimidated and petrified that we lose the courage to act. Lucifer and Ahriman know that when we feel ineffective and useless we are nearly incapable of defending ourselves. And rare are the times when they do not try to make us feel this way. The nerve rattling news with which the media bombards us is enough to shake anyone's confidence. If we recall our feelings when hostages were taken or following a major airline disaster—or even when a neighborhood robbery is reported—the truth of this claim immediately becomes apparent. We feel completely helpless, vulnerable and unable to act.

How are we to counteract these paralyzing feelings? Once again, the answer may be found in the spiritual strength we can gain on the Western path of inner development. We indicated earlier that this path can help us to learn to master our thinking, feeling and will. The steps we take on the Western path that lead to mastery of our feelings help us to conquer fear. If we look at some ordinary situations from everyday life with the insights of this meditative path, we will find that these life situations can serve as illustrations of how to overcome fear.

Imagine you are walking in town and want to cross the street. You look both ways to check that there is no oncoming traffic and you step off the curb into the road. At that very moment— seemingly from out of nowhere—a truck races by and misses you by a hair's breadth. You are frozen where you stand and completely paralyzed by fear. Now let us look at each step you take to overcome this paralysis. The first thing you do is realize that nothing has happened to you, that in reality you are alive and unharmed. Next you will need courage to assess the situation further. By now you have discovered that everything is OK. But without courage you could not continue and decide to make a new attempt to cross the street. Before you step into the road, however, you must first gather will power. Only when you have made the decision to continue and have mustered your will, can you come to act and cross the street.

Let us look at another example. Imagine yourself in each of the following situations. You are climbing high up on a rickety ladder. Your foot slips and misses a rung. Your heart seems to skip a beat and you have a sinking feeling in your stomach. Once more you are paralyzed by fear. Or, imagine yourself hiking on a steep canyon path. Abruptly you lose your footing and accidentally you slide many feet before being stopped by a branch of a tree. You grab that tree, your heart beating wildly. Fear has you in its grip. Think about these situations and you will discover that you always act in accordance with the following four steps:

1. paralysis
2. courage
3. will
4. action

These are the four essential steps we must take to break loose of the paralyzing grip of fear. We are so accustomed to being harassed and feeling defenseless, that proceeding to act often does not even enter our minds. Yet, when we are paralyzed by fear and refrain from action, Lucifer and Ahriman emerge victorious. It is

Ahriman and Lucifer who plunge us into unanticipated situations that leave us paralyzed by fear. Inaction and passivity are exactly what they would like to accomplish with us. Their aim is to render us so paralyzed and weakened that the idea of engaging our will does not even enter our minds. We should never let ourselves be manipulated into such a state that we are paralyzed and do not act. When we are paralyzed by fear we cannot exercise our free will. These four fundamental steps are at the heart of facing and overcoming fear:

1. paralysis
2. courage
3. will
4. action

As a rule we are not conscious that we take these clear-cut steps when faced with fear. However, we must learn to take these steps consciously and systematically if we want to counteract the paralysis by fear which Lucifer and Ahriman create and use against us. This is exactly the reason that we always must keep in mind the essential sequence of paralysis, courage, will, action. When we have made these four steps our own, we only have to recall 1-2-3-4: paralysis - courage - will power - action, and we need never be paralyzed again. We cannot avoid becoming paralyzed by fear, but from then on our responses are up to us. After we have mustered our courage, we will discover that we are already more than halfway home. When we have courage at our command, we are no longer stunned and helpless. We can call forth our will power and take action. The worst predicament in which we can find ourselves is paralysis by fear. Only through our deeds can we break away from this predicament.

For many people paralysis is the consequence—indeed the culmination—of fear. For them, it is the concluding stage from which there is no escape. We now have seen that in frightening situations paralysis by fear should be regarded as a first stage, not the final one. The subsequent stages we must accomplish are courage - will - action. Fear is the invention of Lucifer and Ahriman which keeps us from leading our lives, exercising our free will and proceeding on our path of development. Lucifer and Ahriman hold people in their grip when they succumb to fear and tolerate paralysis as the only response. We must be thoroughly attentive and fully awake each time we find ourselves stuck in a fearful situation. With endurance, perseverance and confidence in our own inner strength, we can defy these circumstances and not succumb.

Unless we build up inner strength we will become puppets of Lucifer and Ahriman. We can build up this inner strength by practicing the meditative spiritual exercises of the Western path. These same exercises help us gain mastery over our thinking, feeling and willing, and attain conscious entry into the spiritual world. They also enable us to cope better with situations of daily life. These meditative exercises can teach us to know ourselves and develop the strength to overcome the unexpected stumbling blocks which Lucifer and Ahriman put on our path.

XIV

The Living Earth and the Moon

In our inquiries we now should turn our attention to what we can find out about the growth of living substance. For example, think of what happens when we trim back a rose bush until it is but a few short stubs. From their appearance we would scarcely believe that there is even a remote possibility of life left in them. Nevertheless, in a few weeks, we can observe on these stems the tiniest beginnings of growth. In a matter of days, these leafy buds will be almost half an inch. And before long many shoots will be several inches. This is only the beginning. Rose buds will appear and two or three days later roses will bloom with stems reaching a height of two feet. This explosion of growth, this expansion of substance is astonishing to observe. We can observe another instance of this when we plant seeds, for example carrot seeds. During the first days after sowing the seeds, nothing seems to be happening. Then, suddenly delicate sprouts of green appear above ground. Several weeks later, we can pull from below the surface carrots the size of a finger. All this growth of substance started with a tiny seed.

An apple tree gives us yet another illustration of growth in the world around us. In spring the tree is laden with blossoms. In summer, the beginnings of fruit can be found where the blossoms had appeared. Between August and October the tree will become overburdened with apples. If the tree is old, we must add support to its branches, so heavy is the weight of the fruit it carries. If we estimate the entire weight of all the apples on one tree, we would be amazed; it would far exceed half a ton. The explosion of growth we observe in the yield of this fruit tree—in only a few months—is altogether spectacular.

The development of an embryo also exhibits this kind of rapid growth. A mouse reproduces a new specimen in two weeks, a human in nine months, a cow in eleven months, an elephant in two years. The multiplication of cells between the conception and birth of a living being is mind-boggling—especially if we also take into consideration the further specialization of cells and their diversification into the various organs. Between conception and birth, the growth that takes place is billion-fold. But this rapid growth does not continue on forever. After birth there is a gradual, yet noticeable retardation of the process. Growth still occurs—but at a slower pace—until the initial stage of development is complete. For example, when an elephant is conceived, the egg cell weighs next to nothing. During the two-year gestation, this first cell multiplies at an astronomical rate until, at birth, the baby elephant weighs nearly two tons. Only a fool would believe that after birth, this baby elephant would continue to expand and develop at the same rate it had in utero. If we were to extrapolate the prenatal growth of this elephant into its first decade of life, our imaginary elephant would come to weigh tens of thousands of tons. We know, of course, that this is not what actually happens. Nonetheless, what we learn from this is that anything living, anything organic, initially undergoes an enormous increase in substance. Then the pace of growth of the organism slows down. This principle governs growth for any living substance.

Imagine we were asked to invent a new human being, starting at the very beginning of its life. How and where would we start? It sounds silly, but let us use this preposterous example in order to make clear our point. When asked to solve this problem, most people would probably design the tiniest little baby, in all form and function a microscopic likeness of the infant they want to achieve. They would allow it time to grow, until it was ready to take its place in the world. That is the way most of us would probably solve this problem. Yet, the reality of the creation of human life is entirely different. During the nine months it takes to bring about a baby that will live on the earth and breathe air, a water-being encased in amniotic fluid is first created. At birth, this baby changes instantaneously from a water-being into an air-being through a remarkable transformation. This process cannot be reversed. The air-being will never again be a water-being. Two immensely important principles of growth are revealed in this illustration. The first is that the transformation from water-being to air-being is instantaneous, coinciding with the moment of birth. The second is that this transformation is irreversible.

Let us keep these two principles of growth in mind—the instantaneous metamorphosis and the irreversibility of the transformation—when we look at the assumptions science makes when it investigates the evolution of the earth. It is unlikely that science would envision creating an air-being—human life—by starting with a water-being. It is just as unlikely that modern science could envision a likewise instantaneous and irreversible metamorphosis resulting in what is known as the planet earth. For the mainstream of modern geological science, the earth could only have come into existence as result of the Big-Bang. For them, the earth is dead mineral matter. Nevertheless, the earth constantly reminds us that it is alive. The earth's inside is teeming with magma. Earthquakes and continental drift also demonstrate that the earth is not merely dead mineral substance. Modern agriculture gradually is coming to the conclusion that soil is living substance which should be treated with reverence and respect. The increasing interest in organic and bio-dynamic agriculture is the result of this emerging understanding of the life of the earth. The earth is a living entity. There are already many outspoken proponents of this notion. The often dramatic work of the Greenpeace Foundation and Friends of the Earth keep this idea in the public eye. There is a growing awareness of the important relationship that exists between the rainforests and the life of the earth. The Gaia Theory proposed by James Lovelock looks at the earth much as a biologist might consider the life of a one-celled organism under a microscope.

Scientists claim that the planet earth is billions of years old. Their determination of its age is based on carbon dating, a process which determines the age of a substance through measurement of its Carbon 14 content, which is known to diminish over time. The calculations which are made using this method seem to be accurate, but, in fact, they are only credible for non-organic, non-living materials. If we could be certain that a substance was never alive, we might be able to rely on the data which carbon dating provides. If, however, the substance is, or ever has been alive, then the results of these calculations are entirely questionable. The measurements that scientists take using carbon dating, and then extrapolate and evaluate, do not take into account the changing rate of growth or decay of a living substance.

Growth is neither linear, nor regular. Living matter first undergoes an explosion of growth in both form and substance, gradually comes to a standstill, and later falls into decay. Because the earth is not dead but alive, it is illogical and even unscientific to speculate on the spectacular developmental stages of the earth as if they have always been linear and regular. If scientists were to carbon date a human baby in the same way they carbon date the earth, they would have to conclude that this newborn would be 500 yards high and weigh thousands of pounds when it reached adulthood. Poor baby. When we finally come to grasp the fact that the earth is a living entity, we will have no choice but to conclude that the accepted calculations of the age of the earth are based on incorrect assumptions.

And now that we have contemplated the earth and the fact that it is alive, it will behoove us to turn our attention to the moon, because the moon has great influence on the planet earth, as well as life on earth itself. What effect does the moon have on the earth? The tides are perhaps the best-known evidence we have of the moon's influence on our lives. It is common knowledge that the level of the ocean's waters rises according to the position and the phases of the moon. In addition, the water table below the surface of the earth rises and falls correspondingly with the waters of the ocean. Thus, the best time to drill a well is at the new moon. If we were to drill at the full moon, we would reach water sooner. Unfortunately, our well would be dry after only a few days.

The menstrual cycle of women is a further manifestation of the moon's influence. The cycle recurs on an average of every 28 days, the same period of time the moon needs to make one full orbit around the earth. Another effect well-known to obstetricians and maternity ward nurses is that more babies are born at or around full moon than around new moon. In addition, mentally ill people are known to react strongly to the moon's cycle. In fact, our word lunatic is derived from the Latin *lunaticus*, meaning moon-struck. Asylum workers know that many of their patients are more difficult to handle at the full moon than at other times. The effect of the moon on these patients is especially strong during an eclipse of the moon, when the moon passes through the shadow of the earth. The disposition of mental patients is known to change as the time of the eclipse approaches. This change is observable even before the eclipse becomes visible—although the patient might be completely unaware of the occurrence of the eclipse. In agriculture, as well, the moon plays a prominent role. Many farmers are aware of the influence of the moon on the growth of crops and plant according to the phases of the moon. Organic and bio-dynamic farmers, in particular, use this knowledge to reap better crops and healthier harvests. Humans are not alone in reacting to the influence of the moon. Hours before a solar eclipse—when the moon comes to stand between the sun and the earth—birds and animals cease to sing or bark and become eerily silent.

From these indications we come to realize that the moon has a profound and far-reaching relationship to life on earth. Why is it that the moon commands such authority over the earth? The answer is simple: The moon was once part of the earth. The fact is that the moon once constituted the very core of the earth. Imagine the authority these same lunar influences must have exercised while the original core was still inside the earth. These influences nearly strangled the potential for life on earth. Just as the human body rids itself of matter it regards as harmful—such as kidney stones—the earth long ago cast out its core. This was a gradual process through which the core (the mass of the earth is eighty times greater than the mass of the moon) slowly was forced toward the surface until a small nodule appeared. This emerging core progressively protruded from the surface of the earth. When the nodule separated from the earth it became what we now know as the moon. Eventually the moon found an orbit in a state of equilibrium with the gravitational pull of the earth nearly 240,000 miles away from the earth.

Convincing evidence that the moon was once united with the earth lies hidden under the oceans. When the earth's core was emerging, it left its marks on the still unstable crust of the earth. When the moon protruded from the earth it created a series of shocks wave over the crust of the earth. These shock waves originated at the location where the core emerged and traveled all over the earth's surface. At a distinct time the shock waves which radiated toward the east, converged with the shock waves which had traveled west. The sites where these waves met, coming from opposite directions, formed mountain ranges and mountainous areas on the surface of the earth, as well as on the floor of the oceans. These sub-oceanic mountain ridges are split by valleys and trenches. These ridges and fracture zones can best be thought of as a continuous band wrapped around the coastlines of the continents. Recently a map of the Floor of the Oceans was published with support of the American Geographical Society and the Office of Naval Research, United States Navy. On this map, these ridges and fracture zones resemble the texture of an elephant's skin. Their formation is consistent and contiguous throughout most of the world. They are the regions were the shock waves met and stabilized. The Arctic Mid-Oceanic Ridge and the Mid-Atlantic Ocean Ridge form a vertical barrier in the Atlantic, situated between the east coast of the Americas and the western coastlines of Europe and the African continent. This ridge then wraps around Africa and Madagascar to meet the Mid-Indian Ocean Ridge, which curves southward to embrace the south coast of Australia and New Zealand, and continues along the entire west coast of the Americas. The shock waves froze at these ridges.

When the Pacific Ocean was fathomed by SONAR, a method which uses sonic and ultrasonic waves to detect the location and size of submerged objects, accurate data on the profiles of this ocean's floor became available for the first time. It revealed that within the Ring of Fire, the sub-oceanic formations are totally dissimilar and unrelated to any other formations, anywhere in the world. The Ring of Fire is a zone which encircles the Pacific Ocean from the west coast of the Americas, across the Aleutians, along Japan, east of the Philippines and New Guinea, north of Australia and New Zealand, and back to the Americas. The configuration, location and size of the mountainous formations inside the Ring of Fire are entirely random. It is not coincidental that this region within the Ring of Fire is where the earth's crust is known to be thinner than elsewhere, and where the volcanic forces of the earth's interior are most likely to surface. It is the region of volcanic and seismic activity unequaled anywhere else on earth.

These unusual configurations in the Pacific are not at all

surprising if we remember that there was a stage during the earth's formation when it was still molten matter. Think of the earth at that time as having the same consistency as a warm pudding. If we would leave a small sphere attached to a thin wire in the center of the pudding when it is quite hot and pull it out when the pudding is nearly cooled, we would be able to produce the same random effect on the skin of the pudding, that we find on the Pacific Ocean floor.

Other evidence that the moon once formed part of the earth was uncovered when the far side of the moon first was photographed. These photographs show that the surface of the moon which is never visible to us, is radically different from the face of the moon, with which we are so familiar. The far side has no seas, only thousands of craters. The surface of the moon which faces the earth is composed of many seas, which we perceive as the man in the moon. Why is it that the near side of the moon is so entirely different from the rear side? We should realize that when the moon protruded from the earth, this emerging core was hot, vulnerable and still fragile. At that time the universe was full of meteorites, which collided with the moon as well as with the earth. Most of these meteorites did not reach or effect the earth, because they burned up in the earth's atmosphere. The moon, however, does not have an atmosphere and was entirely unprotected from the impact of these enormous meteorites. The far side of the moon was exposed to the impact of thousands and thousands of meteors which left their marks on its surface. However, the moon's orbit is such that the same side faces the earth at all times. The mass of the earth—which has a diameter of 7920 miles, more than three times that of the moon—protected and guarded the side of the moon directed towards the earth against the destructive impact of meteorites. The side of the moon facing the earth, therefore, still displays the protruding marks which were created after the separation from the earth. When we compare the side of the moon facing the earth with the hidden side, one distinct conclusion must be drawn: The surface of the moon which is directed toward the earth is the mirror image of the floor of the Pacific Ocean. The submerged mountain range that forms the chain of the Hawaiian Islands is the terrestrial counterpart of the Apennine Mountains on the moon. These areas of the earth uncover unmistakable evidence that the moon separated from the earth at a location in the Pacific Ocean, the center of which is the volcanic Hawaiian island, Mauna Kea.

The moon retains an active and vital relationship to many occurrences on the earth, even though it is in orbit so far away. In order to assure its continued existence as a living entity, the earth needed to eliminate the harmful part of its being—which later became the moon. Had this earth's core remained within, and been allowed to influence further the life of the earth and mankind, human life would have been propelled in a direction entirely contrary to its intended evolutionary course.

XV

CLAIRVOYANCE AND SPIRITUAL DISCRIMINATION

We need further explore the reasons for our existence in a life on earth. We can do this by observing once more the events that all of us will undergo after death. When we enter kamaloka, the realm of desire, we are confronted by every situation in which we were involved during life. Feelings are aroused in us by these situations, but we cannot act on them. Time is perceived, not only in reverse—from death backwards to birth—but three times as fast as on earth. While we are in kamaloka, it will take one year's time—as perceived on earth—to review three years of our past earth life. A simple diagram can explain this. Let us assume someone died in 1986.

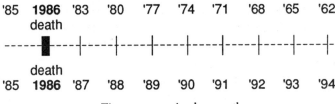

In kamaloka time is perceived in reverse
(3 years experienced in kamaloka = 1 year life on earth)

'85 **1986** '83 '80 '77 '74 '71 '68 '65 '62
     death

death
'85 **1986** '87 '88 '89 '90 '91 '92 '93 '94

Time, as perceived on earth

As the diagram shows, in 1990 this soul will be reviewing his experiences from 1974. In 1991, he will meet the events in which he took part in 1971. And in 1992 he will review the occurrences of 1968. In this way, we can follow approximately the events that a soul—in reality the union of soul and spirit—experiences during kamaloka. If we had a close relationship with a person during life, there are certain disciplines of Western meditation which we can learn and practice to help us empathize with what their soul undergoes after death. While this soul burns off its earthly desires and recalls all the episodes of its past life, it feels the deepest gratitude for our kind, consoling and compassionate contemplations that are the outcome of such meditations. We may also sense the attempts of our friend to communicate with us. There is nothing mystical about this. After all, we are of spiritual origin, clothed in a physical body during life on earth. Normally, we are unaware of their attempts to reach us; nonetheless, they are taking place all the time. If we were clairvoyant, we would be conscious continually of their communications from the spiritual world.

We can discipline ourselves to be attentive to these communications out of the spiritual world. While someone is in kamaloka and occupied with the events of his past life on earth, we are still able to communicate with him. All souls in kamaloka are anxious to have contact with the people they knew during life. As long as there are people on earth with whom they were intimately connected, these souls have access to the physical plane. At times, we can sense intuitively that these souls want to communicate with us. When we recognize a soul in our midst, it is like the experience we have when, from afar, we unexpectedly spot someone we know in a large crowd. The soul is nearly tangible, yet the feeling of its presence is barely describable. It seems this soul is near-at-hand and almost visible, although we know, of course, that this is not physical reality. When this happens, we recognize them, beyond the shadow of a doubt, in the way they express themselves, their manner, and moral characteristics. We—on earth—should become receptive to what these souls want to communicate. If we are making progress on our path of inner development, we can connect with such souls during their sojourn in kamaloka. However, if we are not living a moral life, these souls could shout their revelations to us and they would fall only on our deaf ears. We should be conscious also that spiritual disclosures from souls we did not know on earth will be incomprehensible to us. Such communications would give the impression we were overhearing a conversation in a language with which we were altogether unfamiliar.

People sometimes relate that they were contacted by a relative who had recently died. Others keep such contacts to themselves for fear of being ridiculed. However, a survey for the Chicago National Opinion Research Center, conducted by the theologian Andrew Greeley, indicates that four in ten Americans queried report they have had contact with a relative who died.

Countless souls reside in kamaloka. Each soul had its own life and its own relationships with relatives and friends on earth. During kamaloka each soul will try to contact those people with whom they shared close associations. These souls will persist in their attempts to make contact until they leave kamaloka. At the end of kamaloka soul and spirit separate; the soul merges with the soul-substance of the cosmos and the spirit alone continues into devachan. From then on, life on earth no longer interests the spirit. In devachan, the spirit turns its attention away from earthly concerns and focuses entirely on the spiritual life in the cosmos.

There are also evil souls residing in kamaloka. During their life they were exceedingly devious and threatened the welfare and well being of many people. These souls were so immoral and offensive during life that they must stay an exceptionally long time in kamaloka in order to face all the evil deeds of their past incarnation. Their sojourn in kamaloka could take hundreds of years, occasionally even longer. As long as these evil souls have not yet faced all of their contemptible deeds, they cannot proceed into devachan. While they endure their extended tenure in kamaloka, the people they knew on earth will also die and pass through kamaloka. Ultimately there will be no one left on earth with whom they can relate or communicate. Such souls become more and more isolated. Because these souls are evil and disgusting, they are unable to mirror good souls. But, all souls in kamaloka need social spiritual intercourse and communication. Lonesome and frightened, these evil souls turn to the only contacts still available to them—clairvoyant people on earth. Evil souls who are stuck in kamaloka will use a clairvoyant medium or channeler to establish connections with people they never knew during their life on earth.

There are, and always have been, people who have a certain level of innate, untrained clairvoyance, who can be reached by such beings in the spiritual world. Evil souls know they must conceal their evil nature when they contact these clairvoyants. If their true nature were revealed, it could alarm the channeler or medium and ruin the possibility of further contact with him. Evil souls in kamaloka who make contact with a medium or channeler live simultaneously in two worlds. Part of their existence is in the spiritual world where only truth rules; yet they are still closely connected with the earth, where truth can be manipulated. Because of the dual nature of their existence, these souls still have the potential and the capacity to lie but cannot do so persistently. They know that the way to conceal their evil nature and identity is to minimize the likelihood of awkward personal questions being asked of them.

Were evil souls to connect on a one-to-one basis with a wary and inquisitive individual, questions concerning the true identity of this soul could easily arise. Eventually such souls would have to reveal themselves, their evil nature and intentions. Therefore, evil souls will attempt to divert the medium's or channeler's attention. They tell the medium or channeler that the information they intend to divulge is far too important to be given to one person alone. Evil souls do not want to admit they are evil, even though they are profoundly aware of this fact. Therefore, they instruct their clairvoyant contact that gatherings must be arranged in such a way that it is difficult or impossible for individuals to pose probing or potentially embarrassing questions. They want their messages to be revealed only to a sizeable and receptive audience. They try to impress their audience by speaking in cryptic phrases and riddles. The information they convey seems meaningful, yet puzzling. If anyone in the audience dares to cast doubt on the veracity of the revelations or challenges the identity of these evil souls, they become angry and fly into a rage. If challenged, they will try to scare the hell out of their audience in a further attempt to turn attention away from the truth and the reality of the situation. They bombard the questioner with a barrage of shrieking, personally devastating, ostentatious rhetoric. They try to turn the tables by questioning the motives and integrity of their challenger. Anyone who publicly dares to call into question the integrity of such an evil soul needs to be strong and steadfast—mentally and spiritually—in the face of this virulent tirade. Tremendous courage is needed to expose the dishonesty and unreliability of such evil souls. Unfortunately, in our time, as the incidence of clairvoyance increases, such courage is often lacking. As a result, the real identity of many evil souls who contact human beings through a medium or channeler is never uncovered and misinformation about the spiritual world mounts up.

This does not mean that all information obtained from mediums and channelers is untrustworthy. Nor does it mean that all souls who can be reached through a medium or channel are evil. Most assuredly, good souls exist in kamaloka and are eager to help mankind. Good souls identify themselves readily and openly. They do not object to being questioned. These good souls do not need to manifest only in the presence of large groups of people. Caution must be taken, however, when a soul wants to communicate only with large audiences, particularly when it claims to have died hundreds or even thousands of years ago. Something corrupt and questionable may be going on, because normally a soul does not remain in kamaloka longer than around 30 years. This should serve as a strong warning to us to be wary of such a soul, as well as of the information it brings. When claims are made of having died hundreds or thousands of years before, there can be little doubt that an evil soul—stuck in kamaloka—is at work.

There always have been clairvoyant people, but in our time their numbers arc increasing. Many people who now become clairvoyant experience things they never encountered before. The spiritual images they are able to perceive with this newly acquired clairvoyance make such a deep impression on them, they cannot help but want to share them with others. They soon discover that many people are eager to hear about their clairvoyance. These clairvoyants will share with anyone willing to listen what they believe has been imparted to them out of the spiritual world. The stories they relate of their spiritual escapades sound realistic, true and plausible, which makes it easy for the listener to give credibility to these confidences. This is where Lucifer sneaks into the picture. He loves to tell people about the spiritual world. He does not want them to pay attention to what is happening on earth. The result is that many people—inadvertently—believe these confidences and blindly accept what is presented by these clairvoyants. They regard these clairvoyant revelations as indisputable. There is no doubt in their minds that what has been communicated is infallible wisdom from the spiritual world. Some people are willing even to make changes in their lives and live according to what they have been told. A decision to reshape one's life based on advice from a clairvoyant is not made out of free choice. Were such a choice made as a result of inner growth and progress, it might be considered prudent. Restructuring one's life based entirely on the spiritual disclosures of another is not a free choice. Moreover, it will make the person even more dependent on the one who disclosed the information. Once such a change in life has been made that person will be at the mercy of the one with the clairvoyant visions. From then on, the disclosures of this clairvoyant medium will dominate almost all decisions this person will make in his life.

Lucifer and Ahriman are delighted when we change our life as a result of information and advice imparted by clairvoyants. Lucifer and Ahriman never forget their aim is to make it difficult for mankind to achieve freedom of choice. It is clear they succeed when, instead of making a choice based on the outcome of our own investigations, we docilely submit to what was so indiscriminately presented by a clairvoyant. It is easy to see that once someone has made such a decision, he would continue to follow this same path. To avoid the traps and pitfalls that Lucifer and Ahriman place on our path through these mediums and channelers, we must learn to base every decision about the course of our life on our own freely drawn conclusions.

We always should remind ourselves that the one and only task of mankind is to become free of cosmic law, free of the patronage of the spiritual world. When we defer to information gained by others, we are not free. Instead of increasing our awareness of where we stand in relationship to the spiritual world and the continued evolution of mankind, this mindlessness impairs our ability to personally attain spiritual revelations through inner development. Only through a path of inner development can we attain the insight needed to enter the spiritual world safely. If we have not learned Know Thyself, and are not able to perceive or distinguish the enhancements we have added to our perceptions upon entering the spiritual world, we will misinterpret what we observed. If we have not pursued a path of inner development we will have no way of correctly interpreting what we observe in the spiritual world and we will distort spiritual reality. If then we share our experiences of the spiritual world with others, we think we reveal the truth, not realizing that what we experienced and related to others was a distorted image. Moreover, we are unaware that we ourselves created the distortion. Only when we have learned to recognize the distortion we bring to our spiritual perceptions will we be able to give a trustworthy depiction of the reality of the spiritual world.

When others tell us of their observations in the spiritual world, we actually should be obliged to inquire whether or not they are on a path of inner development and how far they have progressed on their chosen path. Even then, we cannot interpret their communications ourselves, nor have we any way to judge the level of their inner development. How then can we determine that the information they convey is reliable? All disclosures coming from psychics, mediums or channelers must be carefully scrutinized. Only if we are able to reconstruct and verify their spiritual observations on our own, could we trust them. But even then we should not let the clairvoyant make decisions for us. We must make our own choices. Psychics, channelers and mediums may have legitimate insight into the spiritual world. Nevertheless, it is dangerous to rely on what they divulge and to reconstruct our life around their perceptions. As long as we are unable to experience for ourselves the content of cosmic laws, it is best that we keep both feet on the ground and not let the insights of others decide the course of our lives. Even psychics and channelers will tell us not to trust some of their colleagues. If a clairvoyant requires payment for his advice, we should be extremely cautious. Spiritual authorities in the cosmos will have seen to it that someone who can interpret what the spiritual world wants mankind to know will find a profession which will make it possible for this clairvoyant to share his information freely. As soon as dollar signs are related to such spiritual activities, you can suspect Ahriman behind it.

All of us will become clairvoyant in the next decades and centuries as a consequence of the progressing evolution of mankind. Clairvoyance will not be regained by everyone at the same time, but through a gradual process spread over hundreds of years. Just as in the past, when some people lost their clairvoyance before others, there will be people who will regain clairvoyance sooner than others. For this reason, we will be confronted by an ever increasing number of clairvoyant communications from the spiritual world. As we have seen some messages will originate from good souls, others from evil souls. One element in our task of achieving freedom of choice will be to learn to discriminate between the good and evil messages imparted to us. In this new and unfolding stage of our development, we are being tested to determine if we follow unquestioningly the information we receive from these souls. Do we draw our own conclusions and find our own answers from the clairvoyant information which has been disclosed, or do we accept each disclosure at face value? Do we dare to probe the truth of the imparted information, or are we mesmerized by what is prophesied through mediums, clairvoyants and channelers? Have we matured adequately to discriminate between good and evil spiritual communications? Even if we already are able to discriminate between good and evil spiritual communications, are we then also proficient to make decisions about them on our own? Or, if we believe that the information has been transmitted by a good soul do we readily follow the advice it offers?

These are some of the questions that comprise the test of spiritual discrimination we will face, now and in times to come. For mankind today the most crucial challenges and tests lie in this sphere of spiritual discrimination. In this sphere we are presented with a new path, unknown until now, for learning freedom of choice. Our competence to accomplish the task that was given mankind at its inception is being put to the test, once again. This time we are not being judged on abilities we learned in the past. Our mastery of spiritual discrimination will depend entirely upon a code of conduct, which each of us must create for himself. There are no set rules to guide us; only our inner voice, our conscience will tell us what's right or what's wrong. The importance of the answers we are able to offer the spiritual world through the deeds we perform cannot be underestimated.

Moral attitudes and ethics will start to play an increasingly prominent role in the way we will lead our lives. We will no longer evaluate the events taking place around us by mere logic and calculations alone. In our time, in daily life, we will find ourselves confronted ever more with dilemmas which force us to exercise moral discrimination. There are people who have never made a moral judgement or taken a moral stand. They follow the silent majority hoping it will keep them safe from mistakes. As our evolutionary circumstances change, these people will find themselves in situations they have no skills to handle. In times past, survival was based on the ability to persevere. Under the circumstances now arising, each person will have to determine the course of his own future through the development, control and command of moral discrimination.

We are living in one of the most challenging epochs ever. The importance of living in an age that requires the mastery of moral discrimination cannot be overstated. We are confronted with situations which have never before existed on earth. Life was not easy in the past. However, as clairvoyance returns the obstacles on our path will no longer be the domain of the material world alone. The way in which we incorporate moral and spiritual discrimination into our daily life and thinking will have extraordinary ramifications for our future, as well as on our potential to achieve freedom of choice.

XVI

MORALITY, CONSCIENCE,

AND THE

FATE OF THE EARTH

The way we conduct our life on earth is guided by moral customs. We learn these customs from our parents and from the society into which we chose to be born. Throughout history moral customs have changed with every generation. For example, in the eighteenth century slave trading and ownership of another human being was thought to be morally acceptable; in the nineteenth century the keeping of slaves tore the United States in two and was the cause of the Civil War. Today we regard slavery as undeniably immoral. Similarly, the introduction of children into the work force was commonplace during the Industrial Revolution. It was not unusual for factory owners to make contracts with orphanages to employ the children who were housed there. Often adults were fired from their jobs and children hired to replace them because they could be employed more cheaply. Today such treatment of children would be inconceivable in our society—and not just because these practices have been prohibited by law. The moral attitude that permitted such practices to occur had to change before legislation even could be considered. More recently we need only look at the moral convictions of the anti-war protesters, hippies and flower children of the late 1960's and early 1970's to see how moral points of view have changed dramatically even in our own lifetime. Yet, the changes we see occurring today in our cities and towns are even more significant. Street gangs have appeared in our midst that regard human life as less valuable than the life of an insect. Random murders of innocent people are committed daily for no other reason than the joy of killing. The members of many youth gangs regard the taking of someone's life for fun and amusement as completely acceptable. For them, the sadistic and cruel inflicting of pain and bodily harm are pleasurable pastimes. When questioned these young people express no remorse for their cruel deeds; they seem to have no moral feeling or conscience. If we were able to talk to these juveniles about moral customs and issues, they would look at us as if we were talking about life on an other planet. They would have no idea at all what we were talking about. From this we can observe that moral customs do not always change for the better. All this belongs to the decline or progress of earthly morality.

There are distinct differences between earthly morality and cosmic morality. Cosmic morality is spiritual substance and has its origin in the cosmos. Cosmic morality does not change with time or generations; like all cosmic elements it is subject to the unyielding authority of cosmic law. Let us consider the following metaphor in order to more clearly define cosmic morality. On earth we live in air. We cannot exist without the air we breathe. Although we cannot see air, it is around us, nonetheless. Correspondingly, cosmic morality is the substance all cosmic beings need in order to exist in devachan—whether they are spiritual beings which have lived on earth, or spiritual beings that never incarnate. The life-sustaining substance of the universe is cosmic morality. During the period we sojourn in devachan—between death and rebirth—we are sustained by cosmic morality and we accumulate cosmic morality to the same degree we were able to lead a truthful and moral life on earth. We bring the cosmic morality we have acquired with us in the form of our conscience when we return to a new earth life. During the life we live on earth our conscience is the manifested reflection of the cosmic morality we have accrued. Our conscience lies hidden deep within us, however its promptings have an unmistakable influence on our life. Our conscience is part of our spiritual inheritance; it is a reminder of the cosmic morality we have acquired in devachan. In daily life through the exercise of our conscience, every human being is given the opportunity and the ability to metamorphose the morality we are taught on earth and bring it into harmony with the morality that exists in the cosmos. Our conscience should provide the inner ethical and moral reasoning and guidance for all our deeds on earth. It must be clear that we are not talking about deeds performed out of obligation or as a result of external pressure. A genuine act of conscience—however unconscious—is the result of an inner awareness of the truth of cosmic morality and a feeling of responsibility towards the cosmic world.

The results of the harmful and evil deeds we carried out during life are exposed for our individual enlightenment during kamaloka. We are also shown the effects our deeds had on others. We are provided these lessons about ourselves during kamaloka in order to remedy in a subsequent incarnation what we harmed in our past life. But what happens to the good deeds we performed during life? What effect do they have after our death? Do good deeds merely allow us to perfect ourselves, or do they serve a larger purpose? In reality what our good deeds accomplish is remarkable. In order to understand the extraordinary spiritual consequences of what our good deeds accomplish we can consider what occurs when people are kind to one another. When someone treats us with affection, we feel warm and cherished—we glow inwardly, as well as outwardly. When we are kind to someone else—not out of guilt, but when we do so freely, without thought of personal benefit or reward—we create similarly warm feelings in the other person. What are these feelings of warmth and contentment both of us are experiencing? We are conscious that we have these feelings but, in truth, their origin is not in us. The source of these feelings is to be found in the spiritual world. These harmonious feelings are a kind of memory of the warmth in which we were immersed and which we absorbed during our sojourn in devachan. We experience these feelings of warmth and joy because we are beings of cosmic origin and these feelings remind us of the cosmic morality that nurtured and sustained us during devachan.

Sympathies and antipathies, emotions and affections are characteristics that belong only to living beings. The feelings of warmth and affinity we create in others and the corresponding feelings that others inspire in us accumulate in our soul during life on earth. When we die we bring the recollection of the totality of these warm feelings into the spiritual world. Our evil deeds are reflected back to us during kamaloka as lessons about ourselves. However, those deeds we performed out of selfless love inspired by our conscience—those good deeds which were performed as the result of our earthly moral behavior—are metamorphosed into new cosmic morality. This metamorphosed morality is bestowed upon the earth in the form of spiritual warmth which envelopes the earth as a protective sheath. It is the recollection of the warmth of this sheath—which we remember from our sojourn in the spiritual world—that we feel within us when we enact good deeds on earth. This spiritual sheath of warmth—the spiritual mantle created out of the loving thoughts and good deeds of all people— is required by the earth to preserve and foster the planet for its future mission.

We can use a seed as an analogy to more clearly understand what this sheath of loving warmth does for the earth. Imagine that we plant some seeds, place them in the light and warmth of the sun, water them and observe the progress of their development. Some time will pass before any activity will be visible. Then a sprout will emerge which forms the root of the plant. Within weeks or months a fully developed plant will stand before us. If we had kept the seeds in the package in which they were sold none of this activity would have taken place. The life within the seeds would have remained inactive and invisible. A fascinating example of how life can remain dormant and be called into existence only when the proper conditions are provided can be found in the grains that were discovered in the tomb of the Egyptian king, Tutankhamen. These grains were deposited in the mummy chamber as part of the burial ritual of the king over 4,000 years ago. When the tomb of King Tutankhamen was opened in 1922, these grains were brought to the surface and planted. When they were sown out in moist earth and the warmth of the sun, they started to germinate and sprout. Imagine this: for over forty centuries nothing transpired in these grains. Their slumber at last ended when they were put in the appropriate environment of soil, water and warmth. Only when they were placed in the right conditions was their life released to germinate and flourish. Until then each grain had been a sleeping beauty. This sleeping beauty slumbers in every single seed. Each seed holds within itself evidence of one of life's most majestic mysteries. We can observe this mystery manifested in the growth of every living seed.

What is real and valid in the microcosm of a seed is real and valid in the macrocosm, as well. What we find revealed in every individual seed is true for the largest known seed, the planet earth. The earth is the seed for the new cosmos. The macrocosm, as we

know it today, is waiting for the dormant seed—the earth—to germinate and initiate the next stage of cosmic evolution. The development of the earth, like that of all other seeds, cannot begin until the essential and required conditions are provided.

The earth was brought into existence to be independent of cosmic law. This moral sheath of loving warmth for the earth cannot be created by the spiritual world. As a result of the rigidity of cosmic law, high spiritual powers cannot at one moment decree that everything developing on the earth will be exempt from cosmic law and later change their creation by freely granting it cosmic morality. Therefore—in our time—each individual human being must reshape cosmic morality by discovering answers to the moral questions posed by life. During our life on earth, we must mould and modify cosmic morality into a new earthly morality. We can do this only by exercising the free choice we have attained and mastered. We must consciously, actively and freely choose to be moral—out of a genuine love for mankind and the earth. After we die we then render to the cosmos the metamorphosed morality. This metamorphosed and transformed morality becomes one of the most fundamental, essential parts of the spiritual world—the moral sheath of warmth surrounding the planet earth. This moral sheath is a precondition for the evolution of the cosmos, the earth, and mankind.

The macrocosm has perfected the environment for its prospective evolution and created a seed—the earth. The cosmos now anxiously awaits the warmth which is necessary for the seed to germinate. This warmth is created as the spiritual outcome of the good deeds of each individual human being. It is conferred on the earth by each of us at the time of our death. The moral behavior of every single individual—the acts accomplished during life as a result of our conscience—forms the sheath of loving warmth, which initiates the growth and development of the seed, earth. Because of our moral deeds the spiritual sheath of loving warmth will be able to inspire the seed earth to develop into the new cosmos. Only this spiritual sheath of loving warmth can initiate the next stage of the earth's development. When the earth reaches that stage, rigid, ancient cosmic law will no longer rule. A new, independent cosmic law will prevail over the old, unyielding laws, and the new cosmos will be born.

We can now begin to understand the reason why God created the new specimen: man. Mankind is the cornerstone of cosmic evolution. Only mankind is able to transform cosmic morality and achieve freedom of choice. When mankind has gained freedom of choice and established the sheath of loving warmth for the earth, the cosmos will continue the evolution that was interrupted when cosmic law became rigid.

XVII

THE ONE-ELECTRON-MIND

When we observe the human being we see the reality of the physical body. If we were to examine and explore this body, we would have to come to a stunning conclusion: the human being consists of a tremendous variety of organs, each with its own identifying and differentiating characteristic. For example: it is with the eyes that we perceive vision, the ears with which we perceive sound, the skin through which we perceive warmth or cold. There are a great many organs we cannot see immediately because they lie hidden beneath the skin; but the study of human anatomy has familiarized us with many of them, among which are the heart, the liver, the kidneys, the lungs, the glands. The physical body manifests in an amazing variety of organs. The complexity and diversity of what lies hidden below the surface is remarkable. Yet, if we take a closer look, we find something that is even more astonishing. Each organ is built up out of millions of cells, every cell performing a specific task for the whole.

Science tells us that all cells and all physical substance are made up of atoms that are so small they are invisible to the human eye. The development of the electron microscope made it actually possible to observe the atomic image. Atoms consist of a nucleus around which a balanced number of electrons revolve. Let us imagine that we could shrink ourselves until we had become as infinitesimally tiny as one of these electrons. Further imagine that we would retain our full ability to think; that, in actuality, we would become a one-electron-mind. Let us continue our fiction now by envisioning ourselves traveling as this one-electron-mind through the body of a human being. What would we experience? At first, we would have the impression that we were on a journey through a vast, unknown territory. The complexity and variety of what we would find surely would astound us. The human body would seem to be an almost infinite and incomprehensible diversity of unidentified substance. As a one-electron-mind, we might need our entire lifetime to investigate and understand everything we could discover about the complexity and diversity of the human body. Cells and organs, like the heart, liver, kidneys, eyes, lungs, nerves, glands, muscles or skin mysteriously would appear around us. Each mass would have its own unique character, constitution and quality. There would be a tremendous amount of activity occurring in and amongst all of them. Some of these organs would excrete or release matter, either randomly or regularly. Others would swallow substance—what they touched or what approached them would disappear rapidly.

Many of the objects our one-electron-mind would encounter would vibrate in a rhythm specific to each—for instance, the rhythm of the heart would be found to be different than that of the lungs. The activity of some of these objects might seem unrelated to all the others, like the stomach which would appear to set itself in motion arbitrarily. How would we as a one-electron-mind describe and explain the various processes that seem to take place in the human organs? How could our one-electron-mind understand that the activities it was observing within the human body—the pulsating vibration, the rhythmic motions, or the disappearance of matter—were actually the beat of the heart, the movement of the lungs, or the consumption of food. How could our one-electron-mind comprehend that all these organs constitute an integrated totality? Ultimately our one-electron-mind might conclude from the evidence we would gather, that the territory we had observed is an entire universe. Even from an objective standpoint as witness to this adventure, we can easily comprehend how difficult it would be for such a one-electron-mind to grasp the idea that what it is investigating is a living, interdependent totality. Given enough time our one-electron-mind might eventually develop the insight to conclude that this mysterious universe it is exploring is governed by a single—however, physically imperceptible—individual being. Our one-electron-mind would need immense wisdom and imaginative judgement even to consider the larger picture—the reality—and draw the conclusion that this vast universe is governed by this one being, the human ego.

From a cosmic vantage point the earth appears to be no greater in size than a speck of dust. Is not our perspective of the macrocosmic universe similar to that of the one-electron-mind within the living human body? In this macrocosmic universe we encounter a complexity and diversity of matter and substance that is just as mind-boggling as anything our one-electron-mind might discover on its journey within the human body. Astronomy has observed that in the cosmos there are vibrations and rhythms in galaxies and star formations which seem to defy explanation, as well as irregular flickering of light from distant quasars. Science also has discovered locations that swallow substance—what they touch or what approaches them rapidly disappears—and has named these sites black holes. We have already concluded that the earth is the essential nucleus out of which the new cosmos will develop. We can only hope that one day science and mankind may achieve as much wisdom and judgement as we hoped our fictional one-electron-mind would possess. With such insight they could discover that the vast universal territory of the cosmos is governed by one living being. One day they may come to the conclusion that the existing cosmos has created the earth as the seed of what later will become the new cosmos, just as all living beings produce the seed for the next generation. If they were to reach this conclusion, they might be able to take the next steps that would lead to our understanding that with all its complexity, the macrocosmic universe is one integrated, interdependent totality, governed by one being, God. Then all of mankind will come to know that the cosmic universe is the body of GOD.

EPILOGUE: MEMORIES

I shall never see Selma again. She died in Auschwitz in the same gas chamber in which her father and little brother were murdered three weeks earlier. But her eyes I shall always see before me. Selma's eyes have accompanied me since I was sixteen. Why start with what I would most like to forget? It continues to come back to me whenever I try to find a way into life again. So many, many things have happened since that horrific day in 1942.

Hand in hand we sit on the mattress, the last piece of furniture left. The room has a door that opens directly onto the street; it is the only house built that way. Every time I pass this house now, I feel the same throbbing pain in my heart. In this room I looked into eyes so deep, so warm, so overwhelmingly beautiful, I looked into the depths of a soul. Before me I can still see the worn-out carpet and the old mattress on which we sat. Her voice had a deep warmth, not really matching a girl of barely sixteen. I can still recall the smell of her skin. Even now I can feel how her lovely face came to rest in my hands. How cruelly everything had to end. "I am Selma"—that's how you introduced yourself and with these words everything started.

> *. . . very softly I enter . . . you do not notice my presence yet. My eyes slowly glide over you. How I would love to kiss you. . . . Still it is quiet—then you sense the caress of my eyes. You look up—you see me standing there. A smile begins to move over your face. You are glad I am here. We look deep into each other's soul. Your face is radiant. Now you can forget all your sorrow. My hands softly embrace your tender*

*cheeks and lovingly our lips meet. Come sit next to me, as
close as possible. In this way we can sit for ages and forget
everything. Only our two souls exist. Two and yet one, despite
everything. Time comes to a standstill—we do not even notice
it. We are each other and everything is possible. We live just
for one another now. Time is at a standstill. Then the
moment comes I have to part. It is not good-bye—before you
know, I shall be back. Then . . . very softly I enter, you do not
notice my presence yet. . . .*

Like many others I had a job through the Jewish Council to
avoid deportation to Poland. We did not know yet how the system
had been planned by the Nazis. "I am Selma." You asked me to help
you because you were responsible for your little brother and your
father. Like many others you did not know what to do. I had already
seen so many thousands on their way to Westerbork and the
concentration camps during the last several months. But the moment
I saw you something arose in me . . . I knew I had met the woman
of my life.

We saw each other daily. Every evening I could free myself from
work, I came to you. I had a permit which allowed me to be on the
street after eight P.M.; you were imprisoned in your home like all
Jews every evening and every night. When I returned to my parents'
home around eleven P.M. they had already gone to bed, and I had to
heat up my own meal. Everything I experienced during the day I
had to digest alone.

Every night around two A.M., from the theater in which they
assembled their prisoners, the Nazis arranged the deportation of
their Jewish catch to the death camps. During the night there was a
curfew for the whole city so there were no onlookers to witness
their diabolical deeds. Twice daily I brought warm meals to this
theater. Then I had to wait on the theater balcony until the food
containers were empty. From this balcony I could follow what was
happening in the hall below. I remember cabaret performances
given by members of the famous Nelson Cabaret and the Cabaret of
Willy Rosen. These artists were also imprisoned in the theater and
tried to postpone their deportation to the death camps by giving
performances. These men and women were literally playing for their
lives. The absurdity of this ridiculous situation brought us to laughter

on numerous occasions. Gallows humor in the real sense. The performances lasted for hours—no one was in a hurry; everyone welcomed the distraction. The audience was not very demanding—the applause always thunderous. . .

. . . the hubbub was overwhelming, the shouting deafening! We were pressed on top of each other. The pressure from the rear became unbearable—it was almost impossible to breathe. I got stuck and panicked. The guards pulled me over the fence and I took flight. The Beatles performed, and I—who had organized it all—I could not cope with it, and fled. This appearance was the last of a four day tour of Holland. Amsterdam was topsy-turvy. Over one hundred thousand people on the move; traffic came to a standstill, totally disrupted. On the occasion of the visits of Eisenhower, Churchill and de Gaulle the police had less to arrange than with these four English boys. My last conference with the police ended at five A.M. At seven A.M., I was again in the hotel where the Beatles were staying. The moment the boat trip through the Amsterdam canals should have started, the streets were so blocked with people you could have walked their heads. But the Beatles were not there. They were still asleep. The boat trip, a trip which never has had it equal, started half an hour late. The newspapers reported: "Beatles Circus Through Amsterdam."

I had every reason to be satisfied. I had started all this without the slightest idea of how much could have gone out of control, or what misery could have befallen me had even the smallest thing gone wrong. Possibilities by the dozen—a young man jumping from a bridge barely missed crashing his head between the top of the boat and the underside of the bridge. People diving into the canal, trying to climb into the boat, escaping by mere luck the whirling propeller. The boat—upon its arrival—boarded by over one hundred crazy fans, almost sinking it by their sheer weight. The top structure totally collapsed, but there was only material damage. The newspaper headlines read: "Worse Than The French Revolution" and "Fortunately, They Are Gone."

The way all this started still sounds like a fairy tale. A few years after World War II, I followed my technical education with apprenticeships in England—at a radio factory, then at the British Broadcasting Corporation (BBC) and, after that, at a record company. While at this last company I lived at the home of one of their staff employees, a Mr. S. During the war Mr. S' home had been bombed out and both he and his family were evacuated eight times. That clearly could be noticed on their furniture and dishes. Not one part of it matched the other. The meager remains of what once had been a beautiful trousseau was badly damaged; not one plate without a crack or chip, not one cup with a handle. The way they received me and cared for me was beyond compare; I had a lovely time. While I worked at the radio factory, I had seen that they also made plastics. They produced among other things a complete set of dishes made from plastic and I had such a set shipped to Mr. S when my stay with them came to an end. I had given some radio talks for the BBC and I used the money I had earned for this present. I was not around when my gift arrived, but from what I heard later it must have been an unbelievable success. A truck delivered a crate of over 27 cubic feet; it was too big to go through the door. So the crate was opened on the street. Approximately ten different families received parts of the contents. It was amazing how much came out of this crate. Mr. S did not know how to thank me, since in the meantime, I had left for Holland. I had forgotten this matter completely—when twelve years later I had to be in London for a meeting with the same record company, which I now represented in Holland. I was totally surprised when I was received by the same Mr. S, who had climbed the company ladder and now was VP-Export. He was delighted to see me and indicated that at last he would be able to do something in return. He would see to it that the Beatles would come to Holland. "The Beatles, never heard of them." I was only interested in classical music and never had an open ear for pop. Mr. S had to convince me that the Beatles really were quite good, but I had little trust in it.

At my office our staff was delighted. The contract was signed. I lost track of the matter because the visit of the Beatles was postponed time after time, and in the meantime our company had merged with another which managed it. I no longer had anything to do with it. One day Mr. S called from London and informed me of the now definite date of the visit. The Beatles meanwhile had become world famous and were not exactly eager to visit Holland. But a contract was a contract. I felt obligated to Mr. S to ask the new management what they had prepared for this coming event. I was flabbergasted to hear that they were not willing to spend a dime; they said they already had spent too much money on the acquisition of the company and refused to invest any further. I did not want to leave Mr. S in the lurch. So, in the end, I suggested to the new owners that I would finance the visit of the Beatles out of my own pocket, with the condition that I would receive a small percentage from the sale of the records sold within six months. They agreed—all the risks were mine and the probability that I would receive a reasonable amount looked nil. Like me, they could not have presumed that it would become a world success. At the end of the year they had to pay me an amount surpassing my annual income.

I had every reason to look back on an unparalleled success; but instead I was crying bitterly because of undigested grief. The roar and cries of the crowds had carried me back to 1942, to the Jewish Theater. A cabaret performance had been interrupted by the Nazis because they had inserted unexpectedly in the middle of the day an extra deportation convoy to the concentration camps. I had to wait on the balcony and was not allowed to leave before the convoy had left. And so, as a sixteen year old, I had to witness everything which was enacted down below.

One by one the names of those who were to be deported were called out. Every time a name was called, someone got up and slowly slipped towards the aisle where they had to assemble until the convoy was complete. Every time a name is called a shudder weaves through the hall. Everyone hopes his or her name will not be called, that this time the hand of fate will pass them by. But it hits—without mercy—time after time.

From above I can see how, at the calling of a name, someone gets up, says adieu to those around and shifts out of the row like a contagious one, marked, untouchable. Now and then you hear crying, but usually you could hear a pin drop. Anxious, uneasy silence can be felt, interrupted only by the calling of names. It takes hours—for the Nazis want to see that upon the calling of a name, a reaction follows, and the one who has been called takes up his position in the aisle. Suddenly there is a commotion down below. I cannot make out clearly what actually is happening, but in the middle of the hall I see a cluster of people. After a while this cluster untangles again. I do not understand what has happened. Nevertheless a strange tension can be felt. The aisle is now crowded with people; the rows are more than half empty. At last it seems all finished. No names are being called anymore; a certain acceptance can be felt and the German command is heard: "Marsch!" There go the people selected to be slaughtered. The aisle is almost empty now. A heartbreaking scream fills the whole hall and in the flooding silence no one moves. Again the stiff command: "March, quickly!" Then a new commotion and out of a cluster of people a woman is emerging who, crying and shrieking, fights her way across the rows towards the aisle. In the aisle a man and two children are still standing—a boy of about ten and a girl of about eight. To them the woman is heading. This is something which the Nazis cannot allow—panic makes it impossible for them to carry out things according to plan. They command silence. The woman does not even notice. The command is repeated. The woman reaches the aisle and finally everything is back to normal. The mother is able to join her husband and children and the error in the administration is solved. A sharp bang is heard and the woman falls backwards on the floor. The distance between the woman and her family is only a few yards. Then a shouting German commands: "Anyone who moves an inch or comes near the woman will also be shot." Now everything becomes clear. The Nazis claim to be humane. A pregnant woman needs not to be put on the deportation convoy—that is the reason why the family was separated. A heavily pregnant woman should not be put into a freight train; such an action might endanger both mother and child.

I am unable to describe what happened during the following half hour. The crying, dying woman. We see now she is pregnant and that the bullet has penetrated right through her belly. The husband and two children paralyzed a few yards away. The deadly silence. Twenty minutes later the woman was dead. A blanket was put over her. The husband and children were led out of the hall and the convoy left. I got permission to leave and went out.

In this way I was confronted again with the past. Never could I have imagined that the Beatles would bring back this tragedy, which had been suppressed in my memory for over twenty years. You cannot always be prepared for the fact that the past will come knocking, again. Knocking is an understatement—hammering at your brain with a sledgehammer is perhaps more realistic.

In the train she was sitting opposite me—pregnant, with a lovely rounded belly. I could not keep my eyes off her. I did not know her, but I had an immensely strong impulse to place my hands on her belly. To force myself to behave, I sat on my hands. It cost me the greatest effort to resist. At the very first stop I got out. I had to wait several hours before the next train would call at this station, but I preferred that to going through this hell again. I had been in a similar situation previously. An unknown pregnant woman in the street and I *had*, absolutely *h-a-d* to touch her rounded belly. My friends knew this aberration of mine: "Let him be, he does no harm." Via the Beatles I was confronted with this murder in the Jewish Theater. After that it was over.

Even at a distance I saw that things had gone wrong. The doors securely sealed and locked by the Nazis. Selma, her father and little brother taken. I could not sleep that night. The next morning I arrived earlier than usual at my job, to go as soon as possible with my containers of food to the theater. Long before noon I arrived there. I asked someone from the Jewish Council to inform Selma, her father, or her brother that I was in the theater. Selma knew I came to the theater every day and I was certain she would be on the lookout for me. But I did not see her. When I had to leave I was told that her father and brother were on the list of the people who had been deported to Westerbork on their way to the gas chambers that same night. Selma was not mentioned on the list, and therefore she still had to be in the theater. That evening when I came again to bring the food, I was in a state of utmost tension. Why hadn't she been looking for me? I was certain she knew I would be on the balcony. She was aware we would not be able to meet, but at least it would be possible to see one another. But, again, that same evening I could not find her. I simply did not understand. That evening and also the next day I asked if she had been put on a deportation convoy. They assured me that she still had to be there, as she was mentioned on the list of people still remaining in the theater. Wherever I looked and asked I could not find her. Not the next day or the third day or any of the following days. I became desperate and did not know what to do. She was in the theater and had to know that I would be on the lookout for her. For seventeen days I looked for her but could not find any trace of her. Then, on the evening of the eighteenth day, I looked straight into her eyes as I entered with the food containers. Those eyes, that expression I will never be able to forget. That gaze has penetrated me—my whole being—ever since. Eyes filled with endless sorrow, eyes begging to be forgiven. She lay naked in the sentry room of the Nazi guards. We looked into each other's eyes for only a fraction of a second. In this one moment our two souls flowed into each other; our two worlds united. In this same moment our entire world shattered. She was beautiful and young and wanted to live. She had tried to prolong her stay in Amsterdam. She had sacrificed herself so that one last time she could show me that she loved me. In this way! What must have gone through her soul. She—who knew she was lost and, nonetheless, even for only one moment, before the end should come—wanted to see me. That night her willpower broke. That same night she was put on the convoy to Westerbork, then to the gas chambers in Auschwitz where she was gassed a few days later. That night something broke in me. I fell headlong into a deep dark hole. . . .

. . . It is night. Great is my restlessness. Feelings of sorrow, impotence, despair, loneliness and fear block my thinking. A way out I do not see. As cold as a stone am I. The ground on which I stood, taken away. Selma gone. My mind fails to grasp what actually has happened. In total despair I paced back and forth in my hiding place. I am more depressed than ever before. My thoughts keep turning around in circles. If only I could find a way out! Exhausted and beaten I lay down on the bed, too weary to think. Even crying is impossible. Then I glide into a strange world. Around me it is warm. Astonished I see that there is light all around me.

What I saw, I cannot fully remember. I do know that after the infinite feelings of sorrow and fear, suddenly it was light and warm and everything was radiant. It lasted for hours! All around, a world of color. It was pleasant and warm. Not static. It moved; it pulsated.

Warm is the light, eternal the space. Around me many colors, red, and yellow—behind me darkness. In this space I am weightless, without any need. Inconceivable peace, a speck in the distance. I float. I float far away in this endlessness, hardly perceptible. Then I completely fill this eternity. Everything occurs simultlaneously; yet time does not exist. From the darkness I continue to be driven away.

The space pulsates; everything moves, comes nearer, embraces me. I am fully absorbed. Then, again I am far away, unimaginably small in this eternity. The warmth pulsates; the rhythm is calming.

Eternal the warmth,

Eternal the peace,

Eternal the assurance.

The pulsating continues, becomes essence. The light pulsates right through me, radiates red, yellow, then darker. Innumerable nuances the pulsating light reveals, colors unknown to me.

All is warmth,

All is peace,

All is assurance.

It is eternity concealed in form. I am peace. I am eternal. The pulsating space is peace. I become the peace. I am peace. I am eternal.

I am.

I am I.

I am reborn.

When I awoke, I had received the strength to master loneliness on my own for years to come. It has comforted me ever since. I was seventeen.

Robert Van Santen

ABOUT THE AUTHORS

*"One alone can do but little,
but he who unites his strength
with others at the right time. . ."*
Goethe, *The Fairy Tale*

ROBERT VAN SANTEN

Robert Van Santen is well-known in the United States and internationally as a lecturer on a wide variety of anthroposophical and esoteric topics. He was born in Amsterdam, the Netherlands in 1926. As a young Jewish boy of 14 years old he witnessed the Nazi invasion and occupation of the Netherlands. During the war years Robert saw the world crumble before his eyes. His family home was confiscated by the Nazis and his family was forcibly relocated to the Jewish ghetto in Amsterdam. The Nazi occupation marked the end of Robert's formal education—and his entrance into the school of life. In 1942 he and his immediate family went into hiding, each on his own. Nearly a dozen times while underground he narrowly escaped capture and certain death at the hands of the Nazis. His youth was spent witnessing the horrors that war inflicts on the innocent. After the liberation by the Allies in 1945, he found that 90 percent of his family and friends—indeed, 110,000 Dutch Jews—had been murdered in the gas chambers and concentration camps of the Third Reich. The senseless destruction of so many lives haunted him in the years following the war. An autobiographical account of the war years, entitled *Herinnering (Memories)*, was published in the Netherlands in 1980. The ordeals of the war planted in him the seeds of questions about the meaning of death and life, of evil and good that tormented him for more than a quarter of a century, even while he started a family and a highly successful career in business—which among many ventures included ownership of an electronics sales company and organizing the Beatles' famous tour of Holland in 1964. Robert Van Santen served for more than a decade as President of the Dutch national sales organization for electronic products.

For 15 years, in his capacity as Secretary Robert Van Santen promoted and organized the prestigious *Oskar Back National Violinist Competition* in Holland. In addition, he developed a career of his own as an internationally acclaimed Master Portrait Photographer. His photographs have been exhibited in museums and galleries in Holland, London and the States. He has acted as a jury-member for the *Reader's Digest's* photo competitions.

His questions about the meaning of life, and his life-long struggle with the consequences of WWII led him to anthroposophy. The insights and answers that anthroposophy offered brought about a consequential decision in 1980. Robert liquidated his business in Holland and emigrated to the United States. Shortly after his arrival in the States he was elected President of Rudolf Steiner College where he served for two years. He has taught classes on an extensive range of esoteric and anthroposophical subjects in both public and private colleges, and lectured to enthusiastic audiences from coast to coast. A serious illness in 1987 curtailed these activities and left him with insufficient strength, but a powerful resolve to write down the content of his thoughts on the meaning of life.

MARGUERITE MILLER

Marguerite Miller was born in Detroit. A quiet, Midwestern childhood in the 1950's provided the foundation for her life. But like many of her generation, it offered little preparation for the events she would face as a young woman in the 1960's. The death of an infant brother focused her attention on the questions about the meaning of life and death that had troubled her for as long as she could remember. The tumult of the Civil Rights riots of the late 1960's and the turmoil of the Viet Nam war years helped her further to formulate these questions and actively begin seeking answers. For years the soothing logic and balance of mathematics fascinated her, and it was there she first sought answers to life's riddles. At the same time a long standing interest in words and languages lead her to a college German course which required her to read Goethe's *Faust*. It was there she realized that the answers to her questions never would be found in numbers and figures. As a result she went on to earn both a bachelor's and a master's degree in 19th century German literature from the University of Michigan. Through her studies in German literature and the friendships she formed, Marguerite found anthroposophy and the work of Rudolf Steiner. Marguerite has served as a member of the Board of Directors of the Rudolf Steiner Institute of the Great Lakes Area. She also was editor of the *Directory of Initiatives of the Anthroposophical Society in America*. Currently she divides her time between raising a family and writing.

Robert and Marguerite have known each other for several years. Their creative collaboration began in 1988 when Robert returned from his surgery and was unable to lecture or travel. When he began work on this book, Marguerite expressed interest in the project. Their creative co-authorship was thus founded in spite of the thousands of miles separating them. A second book on the Western path of inner development is in the works—again written in a true co-authorship.

GLOSSARY

This glossary is intended to be used as a reference for some terms used in this book. It also can help the reader further understand the concepts presented throughout the text. The definitions found here are not meant to apply to the same expressions or words used in other books or in different contexts.

AHRIMAN
The exalted spiritual being which has the task of challenging humanity to achieve freedom of choice. Ahriman does this by creating circumstances that might lead mankind to believe that its purpose can be found only on the physical plane, the earth. Ahriman tries to persuade man that a spiritual world does not exist, that man has no spiritual component, and that all time spent in pursuit of a spiritual life is wasted. Ahriman conceals his presence and his activities from mankind by working in close connection with Lucifer. See also LUCIFER.

AHRIMANIC ENTITIES
Lesser spiritual beings aligned with Ahriman and his role in human life.

ANTHROPOSOPHY
Literally: "wisdom of man." The philosophy articulated by Rudolf Steiner between 1900 and 1925. Anthroposophy explains the influence of the spiritual world and its inhabitants on life on earth. Anthroposophy encompasses a new perception of human life, education, agriculture, the arts, sciences and philosophy.

BIRTH	The transition from the completely spiritual level of existence to the level in which a physical body is acquired.
CHANNELER	A human being who acts as a passive conduit for communications from a spiritual entity in the spiritual world. The channeler is used by this spiritual entity to disclose messages to human beings living on earth. See also MEDIUM.
CLAIRVOYANCE	The ability during life on earth to discern aspects of the spiritual world, spiritual beings residing in the spiritual world and certain influences they may exert on human existence.
CLAIRVOYANT	One who possesses the faculty of clairvoyance.
CONSCIENCE	The spiritual force which guides man's moral deeds during life on earth. See also MORALITY and COSMIC MORALITY.
COSMIC MORALITY	The spiritual element which sustains all life in the spiritual world. Cosmic morality is absorbed by the human spirit during its sojourn in the spiritual world in proportion to the level of morality this human spirit was able to attain during its most recent life on earth.
COSMIC LAW	The unavoidable, immutable laws that govern the spiritual world. All beings in the spiritual world are bound by and must abide by these laws.
COSMOS	Infinity and all that exists within it, encompassing the spiritual world as well as our solar system. See also SPIRITUAL WORLD.
DEATH	The transition from the physical level to the spiritual level of existence in which the physical

body is laid aside.

DEVACHAN The quintessential spiritual world to which the human spirit returns after it has passed through death, panorama and kamaloka. Evil does not exist in devachan.

DOUBLE The evil and hideous spiritual counterpart of every human being which is a result of the individual's harmful deeds enacted during former incarnations. The double is composed of ahrimanic entities that cannot incarnate on their own. The double resides within the soul and accompanies each human being from before birth until the moment of death.

EARTH The planet which was developed and prepared especially for human life. The earth was made exempt from cosmic law so that man could accomplish the individual and cosmic tasks of creating freedom of choice, for which mankind was created.

EARTHLY MORALITY The reflection during life on earth of the cosmic morality which was absorbed by the human spirit during its sojourn in the spiritual world. The degree to which man is able to put into practice this earthly morality during his present life on earth determines the level of cosmic morality that he may achieve and acquire after death—which then will influence his moral stand in his next life on earth. See also COSMIC MORALITY and MORALITY.

EGO The eternal part of man which advances from incarnation to incarnation. Ego and spirit are in reality the same. During life on earth this eternal entity is called ego; in the spiritual world after death it is called spirit. The ego is the eternal entity which guides man through his journey during life on earth. See also SPIRIT.

GUARDIAN OF THE THRESHOLD

A spiritual being which has many tasks and countenances. One of its fundamental tasks is to test the human being's level of preparedness for entrance into the spiritual world during life on earth. When a human gains passage into the spiritual world the guardian of the threshold will stand before him to safeguard him until he is secure enough to withstand the perils and hazards of the spiritual world. The guardian of the threshold typically has the frightful and shocking countenance of the individual's double. See also DOUBLE.

INCARNATION

The process of acquiring a physical body to clothe the ego, in preparation for life on earth. The term incarnation is also used to designate the phase of life the human being experiences after he has descended from the spiritual world.

KAMALOKA

One of the principal stages in the spiritual world each human must experience after completion of a life on earth. The duration of kamaloka is approximately one third the length of the recently completed life. During kamaloka the individual perceives all the consequences of the deeds it enacted during life on earth. These consequences are viewed in reverse order—from death until birth. In addition, the individual perceives the results of his own deeds in a manner comparable to the way other people endured these deeds.

KARMA

The spiritual law of cause and effect. Karma determines that the deeds an individual performs during one life on earth have irrevocable repercussions in his subsequent incarnations.

Through the exercise of free choice the human being is able to modify his karma in his present life.

KNOW THYSELF
The elevated state of inner, spiritual development the human being needs to attain in order to achieve a safe passage into the spiritual world during life on earth.

LUCIFER
The exalted spiritual being which has the task of challenging mankind to grow and develop. Lucifer does so by trying to convince mankind that its task is to be found only in the spiritual world and not on the earth. Through his activity Lucifer emphasizes the supremacy of man's spiritual existence, and tries to lure man away from his task on the physical plane. Lucifer conceals his presence and activities from humanity by working in close connection with Ahriman. See also AHRIMAN.

MEDITATION
A practice of spiritual reflection and exercise for the purpose of making a connection to the spiritual world.

MEDIUM
A human being who acts as a passive conduit for communications from a spiritual being dwelling in the spiritual world. See also CHANNELER.

MORALITY
The accruing sum of an individual's beneficial deeds during this life as well as former lives on earth. Cosmic morality is absorbed by the human spirit during its sojourn in the spiritual world in proportion to the level of earthly morality it was able to attain during its most recent life on earth. Earthly moral deeds are influenced by resolves made during the sojourn of the spirit in the

spiritual world. See also Cosmic Morality and Earthly Morality.

NIRVANA

The Sanskrit term for the state of release of the eternal part of the human being, accomplished through the extinction of the self. Nirvana terminates the sequence of pain and suffering and the endless cycle of lives on earth as described in Oriental philosophies. See also Satori.

PANORAMA

The transitional episode between death on earth and the entrance into the spiritual world. During panorama the most recently departed life is reviewed in colorful images. However, these images evoke no feelings in the individual. The duration of panorama is approximately three days.

PAST-LIFE REGRESSION

The result of a variety of techniques which induce in the human being recollection of pre-birth experiences, and activate memories of encounters and events from former lives.

PATH OF INNER DEVELOPMENT

An individual process of spiritual exercise and reflection which may result in an increased perception of or conscious passage into the spiritual world during life on earth; closely related to meditation.

PREDESTINATION

The idea that every occurrence in life is preordained and that the irrevocable course of events cannot be modified by human intervention.

REINCARNATION

The concept of human beings returning to the spiritual world after death, where they prepare for a subsequent rebirth and earthly human life.

SATORI

A condition described in Oriental philosophies in which all worldly images have left the individual and an ultimate level of inner peace and unity with nature is attained. See also NIRVANA.

SOUL

The spiritual essence in which the ego envelops itself for its sojourn during life on earth. The soul serves the ego as interpreter of the events of earthly life and translates the impressions of outward life into emotions and feelings for the ego. After death the soul will remain united with the spirit until all its earthly impressions have been endowed to the spirit. See also EGO and SPIRIT.

SPIRIT

The eternal part of man which advances from incarnation to incarnation. The spirit guides the human being through its journey in the spiritual world. Spirit and ego are two names for the same eternal entity. Ego is used to designate it during life on earth; spirit is used to designate it during its existence in the spiritual world. Although the spirit is eternal, it grows and evolves as a result of deeds performed during life on earth. See also EGO.

SPIRITUAL WORLD

The region within the cosmos from which all life originates and to which—after death—all life returns. See also COSMOS.

WHEEL OF INCARNATIONS

The portrayal by Oriental philosophies of man's existence as a vicious circle of incarnations, deaths, and reincarnations. According to these Oriental philosophies the human being is bound endlessly to the wheel of incarnations as long as he clings to the illusion of the importance of the self. When man is able to break the spell of this illusion, his eternal part is released and the self is extinguished. As a consequence the sequence of pain and suffering of repeated lives on earth is concluded, the cycles on the wheel of incarnations are completed, and Nirvana is achieved.

INDEX